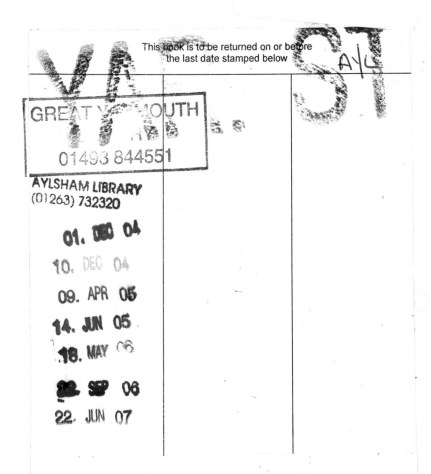

THE BANVILLE DIARIES

Portrait of Larry Banville, painted in the autumn of 1843 at Northrepps Hall.
'Its appearance almost frightened me,' Larry wrote.

THE BANVILLE DIARIES

DIARIES

Journals of a Norfolk Gamekeeper
1822–44

Edited by
Norma Virgoe and Susan Yaxley

Introduction by
LORD BUXTON

COLLINS
8 Grafton Street, London W1
1986

William Collins Sons and Co. Ltd
London · Glasgow · Sydney · Auckland
Toronto · Johannesburg

LBAN

350834

First published 1986
© The Banville Diaries and introduction Aubrey Buxton 1986
© Editorial selection, transliteration and linking texts Norma Virgoe and Susan Yaxley 1986

Banville, Larry
The Banville diaries : journals of a
Norfolk gamekeeper, 1822-44.
1. Gamekeepers—England—Norfolk—
History—19th century
I. Title   II. Virgoe, Norma   III. Yaxley, Susan
639.9'5'0924   SK505
ISBN 0 00 217634 3

Photoset in Linotron Old Style by
Rowland Phototypesetting Ltd,
Bury St Edmunds, Suffolk
Printed in Great Britain by
Butler & Tanner Ltd, Frome and London

CONTENTS

INTRODUCTION

I HAVE KNOWN ABOUT the Banville diaries since childhood, and I spent much of my school holidays over fifty years ago in the company of Larry Banville, a much loved family figure. He was not the author of these diaries but his grandson, who still worked for the family until after the war. It was unusual that two families were so close for nearly 150 years.

The first Larry Banville's will when he died in 1869 dictated that Charles Buxton, a younger son of his late employer, should be given 'all and every my Diary Manuscripts and Papers which I wish to be published'. So it was always his intention that the world should read his intriguing records and revelations. Now, thanks to the dedicated endeavours of Norma Virgoe and Susan Yaxley, his wishes are finally being fulfilled.

Small extracts have appeared before in various books and publications, usually in connection with the re-introduction to this country of the then extinct capercaillie. North of the border it has always been held by the sporting fraternity that the capercaillie was re-introduced to Scotland by Lord Breadalbane at Taymouth, and that was that. I remember once at a shooting party in Aberdeenshire many years ago being bold enough to proclaim that the capercaillie had been introduced by my great-great-grandfather who had sent his keeper from Norfolk to Sweden to collect the birds. All Hell broke loose over the breakfast table and I was practically laughed out of court. 'Breadalbane!' they bayed, with scorn and disdain.

Now, however, the man himself describes for all to read his epic trip from Cromer, embarking at Harwich and sailing in exceptional discomfort and feeling seasick, spending weeks in Sweden collecting the birds, crating them up, and then sailing with equal hardship back to Dundee, finally to release the birds with Breadalbane's keeper at Taymouth. Buxton had enjoyed handsome hospitality at Taymouth and decided to repay his host by this unique gesture. The 'capers' did well and multiplied everywhere.

The diaries have remained with the family since Banville died, except for a period after the war when they were looked after by the daughter of Larry the Third, Jean Gough. Mrs Gough very kindly handed them back to me in the 1960s and more recently I initiated the publishing exercise by engaging the interest of our two editors. The diaries are now here at Stiffkey only a dozen miles from where they were written with such perseverance generations ago.

They are, of course, too long to publish in full. The editors have been ingeniously selective from the two thousand pages and have succeeded in giving a vivid flavour of the different aspects of Banville's life and interests, mainly in North Norfolk. The task which the editors faced was a daunting one and can be judged from the following interpretation. Banville wrote:

'I went in to Holt to Mr. Randalls the watchmaker to see if He got me a Pear of Barls from manstearter when I was there we had some astrs to Eat we also had som Bear with Mr. Wust Mr masts keeper From Barningham Hall.'

The editors have translated it thus:

'I went into Holt to Mr. Randall's, the watchmaker [and gunsmith] to see if he got me a pair of barrels from Manchester. When I was there we had some oysters to eat. We also had some beer with Mr West, Mr Mott's keeper from Barningham Hall.'

But for the editors it was nothing like as easy as that. Larry was virtually uneducated, and although his hand had become fluent when he copied out his notes, it would have been a laborious struggle for any of us to decipher accurately even this short passage. By at first deciphering and later mastering Larry's idiosyncratic hand, the editors worked tirelessly through the four volumes.

These records of a gamekeeper span the years 1822 to 1844. During his working life he saw great changes in the shooting scene, and in the early days he would walk up game every day with the members of the family staying in the house, with two or three keepers and probably staff to replenish the muzzle loaders. The quarry was all wild game birds, nothing was reared, and one of the most telling factors for us today is that there were always far more partridges than pheasants. The records reproduced here show this clearly.

Later in the 19th and 20th centuries the steady erosion of wild country by development, the rapid spread of roads and tarmac, the drastic improvements in agriculture, the completely pointless spraying of banks and hedges, and finally the custom of entertaining guests at shoots when breech loaders became the fashion, resulted in the partridge/pheasant situation being critically reversed. There was simply not enough wild unspoilt country left, with rough areas, banks and heaths to sustain wild partridges in large numbers, whereas pheasants, an introduced species, are as easy to rear as poultry in any sort of landscape. Today there is hardly a handful of manors in East Anglia where wild partridges are still conserved in any quantity.

In Larry's day a hundred and fifty years ago, wild habitat did exist on a considerable scale, although the writing was on the wall even then. It did not occur to most people in those days that populations of wild species were not infinite. The natural world was there to be shot and collected whether game or wildfowl, a bittern or an avocet. The notion that there might be a limit to the punishment that natural populations could sustain was only conceived by a handful of pioneers in conservation. More than a century later the wild partridges had succumbed to a drastic extent.

It was largely the shooting that lured the Buxtons to North Norfolk. The main family home was always in Essex, and they only rented houses in North Norfolk, first Cromer and then Northrepps. While Essex was home, all holidays and every conceivable opportunity were spent on the Norfolk coast, a habit which has been pursued by succeeding generations. T. F. Buxton and his brother-in-law Sam Hoare rented or bought all the shooting they could lay their hands on, from Weybourne in the west to Trimingham in the east, and for some miles inland. It was an immense area, about the size of the famous principality of Holkham.

Renting this great sprawl along the coast enabled the family to go out day after day, week after week, during the Parliamentary recess, with just the household invariably making up the party. There was no driving of game and no beaters, just Larry and the other keepers. When breech-loaders eventually came in they discovered that good driven shots were more fun than walking up. Pheasant-rearing started and then game-shooting swiftly evolved into the conventional set-piece routine as the sporting fraternity knows it today.

After reading Banville, it is poignant to drive along the North Norfolk coast today and, except for the loss of wild country, to feel how remarkably the scene is unchanged in general character. Cromer Hall was rebuilt after a fire in 1829, but Northrepps is unaltered. Gunton has finally passed from the Suffield family, but the house has been restored by a new owner. Felbrigg Hall has been left to the National Trust for all to see and enjoy today. The last Upcher at Sheringham Hall died only last year in 1985, but Humphry

Repton's enchanting house and landscape are still as they were when Charlotte Upcher, who figures so much in Banville's diaries, was the very becoming widow about whom, incidentally, he made insinuations. Banville records in his diary that she decided out shooting to load the muzzle-loader for his master, and then inferred from that that there was a bit of an affair going on between them. This is preposterous. Today, if every time a woman offered to load for a man out shooting she was suspected of having an affair, the shooting field would indeed be a risky scene for us all.

Was Larry an outrageous gossip, an incurable prude, or conceivably a shrewd and critical observer? Or all three, and a bit more? There are other rather coarse and sometimes vulgar observations in the diaries about Lady Breadalbane, Thomas Coke of Holkham, the Windham daughters, and many others who caught his sharp eye for satire or journalistic licence. Larry's motives will probably remain an enduring enigma.

Round about the area today one cannot help reflecting as well about the old manors, where Banville and the family tramped the rough land, the woods, and the small fields. All the hamlets and manors are there on the signposts, as they are in the diaries and gamebooks – Weybourne, Bodham, Beeston, Runton, Gunton, Beckham and Felthorpe. Although things are very much changed to the eye, to the mind they are hardly changed at all. Particularly fascinating for me are Larry's wildfowling expeditions to Stiffkey sluices, because it appears that he and his fellow keeper Parsons used to crouch in the creek to shoot duck and geese at the very place where I now keep my boat, at the mouth of the Stiffkey river. Whether they ever used a gun punt he does not say, but obviously he loved his trips to the marshes and saltings at Stiffkey, and to the wetlands to shoot snipe at Barton in the Broads.

Those who do not want to read only about shooting and gamekeeping will not be disappointed with this book, because the diaries are primarily about people, about the varied community who lived in this much loved area, as well as revealing observations on the inhabitants in Sweden and Scotland and all the places along his travels. Banville's writing conveys more vividly than history books the true distress caused by the Corn Laws and the Game Laws, and the fearful plight of widows left with children but no means of subsistence at all except the most pitiful levels of charity. His daily notes were about neighbours he knew in Cromer, Sheringham, and all the villages, in a period when there was great distress among farmworkers and the agricultural community. It is painful as well to read about the plight of seamen and sailors in storms and shipwrecks, where the names and the circumstances are described.

One can clearly detect through Banville that the so-called gentry were split by temperament and outlook. In North Norfolk the Buxtons, Hoares and Gurneys were deeply uncomfortable about poverty and injustice, and became notable reformers. One sister-in-law was Elizabeth Fry, a Gurney sister of Hannah Buxton and Louisa Hoare. Their grander neighbour Lord Suffield was also strongly opposed to the Game Laws and thought that they should be abolished. He was in fact their reforming partner in the House of Lords and was regarded as a somewhat embarrassing rebel by his relations.

On the other hand the Windhams of Felbrigg, who Banville considered thoroughly pompous, did not believe in change at all. And as a landowner Admiral Windham, who changed his name from Lukin to inherit the estate, obviously despised Buxtons and Hoares who merely rented properties for sport, possibly as some Scottish lairds might feel today about their grouse-shooting tenants from the south and abroad.

Banville has performed one important service for the Norfolk families with whom he was involved, he has set the record straight. The Buxtons and Gurneys spawned a profusion of literature on reform, philanthropy and emancipation of the slaves, all of which conveyed the impression for over a century that our forebears tended to be pious prigs permanently on their knees. Some descendants, mainly elderly aunts, would have canonized the first baronet if they had been given half a chance. I discovered early symptoms of this emancipation mania in a letter I found from a 19th-century Buxton lady who wrote with ill-concealed irony, 'Uncle evidently prefers to pray whilst leaning on his gun.'

It would be ridiculous to belittle the historical achievements of the reformers of the day, but one does not have to pretend that they were saints. It is somewhat reassuring for less worthy descendants to discover through Banville that Buxton, Hoare and their cronies were fundamentally normal. They worked like blazes at their causes in Britain and in Africa, and the winning of major reforms in Parliament was greeted with as much acclamation as a Cup Final. But they had their breaks in the recess like everyone else and became typical inhabitants on leave in Norfolk, living as people do in the county. Even the most fervent reformers and visionaries are inspired to identify themselves with North Norfolk, in a manner consistent with the whims of the wild heaths, the sands, the marshes, the sea, the winds and the sky.

Those wonderful skies would keep anyone normal. They are well conveyed by some of the fine paintings reproduced here from the Norfolk School, which demonstrate clearly the changes in wildlife habitat in the 19th and 20th centuries. The views along the coast show starkly how the fields and heaths have since been overwhelmed and obliterated. These popular places, once self-contained little coastal towns and fishing ports, are today sprawling holiday resorts, much loved by visitors from afar and especially from the Midlands.

Most of the portraits in this book are by George Richmond, the Victorian academician, who painted so exquisitely in water-colour, and who spent long periods over twenty years with this particular North Norfolk circle. Although its members had been his primary patrons, he did not invariably appreciate their hospitality. Describing one visit to Northrepps, Richmond, obviously a sensitive and fastidious person from the metropolis, implied that his quarters were not completely comfortable, mentioning a 'detestable smell of mice' in his room. He wrote 'what with birds and beasts in this house the air is not fit to breathe; how little people seem to value fresh air when they are surrounded by it'. I am glad to say that in my household today the night at bed-time reverberates with the sound of windows being flung open wide. The birds referred to were presumably skins collected by Banville for the Buxton boys, who were already showing signs of becoming keen ornithologists as well as shots. The beasts were no doubt the family dogs.

The fine traditional bird pictures by Archibald Thorburn and one by Woodhouse were painted later than the years of the diaries, but they are wholly appropriate as a component of this book. Wild species do not after all change their plumage like human beings from one century to another. The wide landscapes in the paintings, of partridges in particular, relate directly to Banville's text and reflect the open countryside portrayed by the Norfolk School.

I am delighted that Banville's diaries are now at last for 'the public to see' and I congratulate the editors and the publishers on their very satisfying achievement. Larry was certainly a remarkable character and this book holds pleasure and interest for everyone.

Stiffkey, Norfolk   AUBREY BUXTON

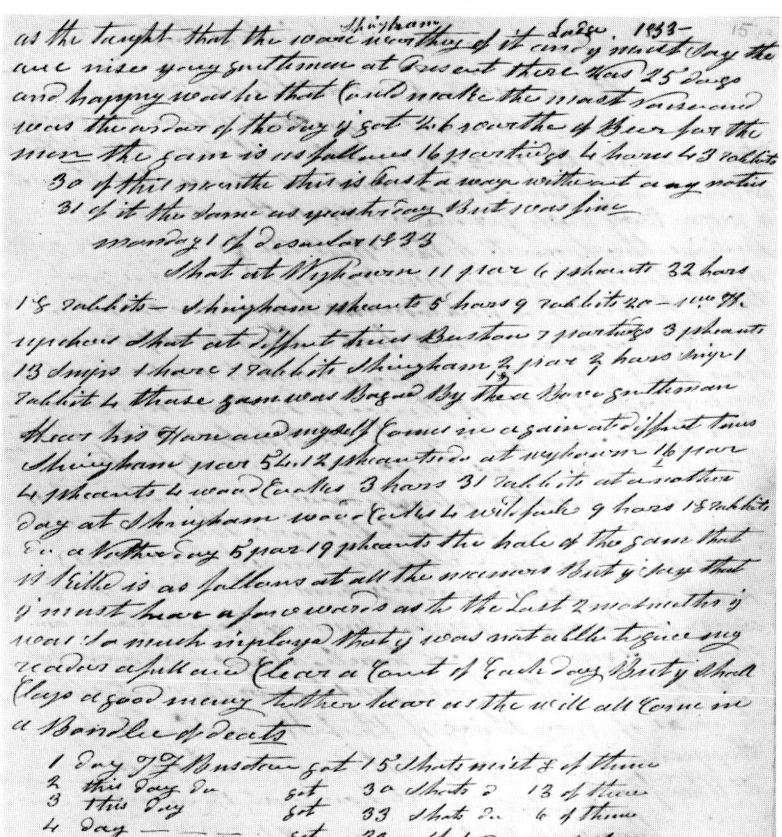

A typical diary entry, dated 1833.

CHRONOLOGY OF
BANVILLE'S LIFE

1796		Birth in Cullenstown, County Wexford.
1822	July	Leaves Ireland with Llewellyn Lloyd.
	Autumn	In Yorkshire and Scotland.
1823	August	Enters the employment of Thomas Fowell Buxton who sends him to Norfolk.
1824	July	Sails to Sweden with Llewellyn Lloyd.
1825	June	Returns to Norfolk.
	December	Marries Sarah Lown.
1829	March	The Banvilles move into the Sheringham lodge.
1836	February	Visits Ireland.
	August	Shooting in Scotland.
1837	April	Second visit to Sweden.
	June	Returns to Scotland with the capercaillies.
	September	Period covered by the missing pages of the diary during
1841	September	which Banville again visits Sweden.
1843	February	Journey to Windsor.
	April	The Banvilles move to Runton.
1844	May	Diary ends.
1845	February	Death of Sir T. F. Buxton.
1869	March	Death of Banville.

'Red Grouse' by William Woodhouse.

PART I

THE MAKING
OF A GAMEKEEPER

1822–1826

Typical gamekeepers of the period. The Buxton keepers wore dark green coats and brass buttons, but possibly Larry was usually too independent to wear 'uniform'.

———— ⋯⟫⟫▭⟪⟪⋯ ————

Chapter One

LLEWELLYN LLOYD

1822–23

'It was in a town of the name of Cullenstown in the County of Wexford I was born, of honest parents although they were poor, which was no sort of disgrace to them. Her name was Biddy; her maiden name was Ryan. My father's name was John Banville, a weaver . . .

My father he had 7 children all was sons and my poor mother died when we all were of a tender age which left my tender father in great grief. He strove to rear all of us up in the fear of God . . . My father never married for he always said that no woman should come in to supervise his children.'

These are the opening words of the diary of Laurence Banville, 'Poor Larry' as he frequently called himself in later years.

He was born in 1796 in a rural area of Wexford, which was then one of the more prosperous counties of southern Ireland. He says nothing of any formal education, but he obviously learnt to read and to write a fair hand. His spelling and punctuation were atrocious, but his arithmetic was usually reliable. His fierce pride, so evident in the opening words of the diary, was clearly inbred and, despite spending his whole working life as a servant, he never lost it.

This pride may well provide the answer to the enigma of why a young Irishman such as Banville should have felt the need to keep a daily diary for at least twenty-two years and possibly longer. He loved to record his travels and exploits and those of his masters, particularly in the bagging of game. He also felt driven to describe, with some passion, the injustices he suffered at their hands, believing always that some day his words would be read with sympathy and understanding.

'I do intend to lay before the public . . . a few of my trials and travels and how some gentlemen treated me and who I am in debt to for my rising in the world.'

Although his formal education was limited, young Larry acquired the usual skills and local knowledge of a country boy and was able to make himself useful to two local landowners, the brothers Joseph and William Goff.

'I was always very apt to find birds' nests and also bees' nests. I had a dog of the name Whiskey that would hunt the ducks and bark when he would find one and I used to go out with my father to find hares and rabbits sitting in their forms which I shortly became apt at it . . . I believe I was about 13 or 15 years old at that time, at least I was so young that either of them used to carry me behind them on horse-back out to the sporting ground and always thought that they would not have sport unless I was with them . . .

I then went and hired with Mr William Goff for the sum of £8 a year and no clothes, but if his son, Mr Jacob Goff, wanted me to go any place with him he was to get me some clothes. He was a fine young man. He behaved very well to me. I lived 3½ years with them; during that time I was furnished with a waistcoat, coat and hat which was as livery with his crest on the buttons, which I thought myself not accountable for . . .

When I went to settle, Mr William charged me for the clothes which was about £6. 10s. and also charged me for a coat made me a present and a britches that he also said he gave me. He bought them for £1 and he charged me £1. 10s. . . . In all he wronged me of £17. 4s. 10d. which was too much for me to lose . . . I hope and trust that these few lines will be a warning to all young fellows that will them see.'

Soon after this, in 1822, Banville entered the service of Llewellyn Lloyd, a young gentleman from a Montgomeryshire family. The Lloyds had made a great deal of money from the iron industry in the 18th century and Samson Lloyd, Llewellyn Lloyd's grandfather, was a renowned Quaker banker in Birmingham. His father, John, was also a banker, but Llewellyn, born in 1792, the fifth and youngest son, was not well off and clearly found some difficulty in financing his consuming passion for hunting and shooting. He offered the young Irishman the excitement and adventure of foreign travel, but no salary. Perhaps influenced by the poor prospects for employment in Ireland, Banville agreed to this on condition that Lloyd found a good position for him on his return.

'15 July 1822
I left my own country. I sailed away from Duncannon to London. On my way I saw the French land and also the coast of England. I then came to

London where my master Mr L. Lloyd sent me to a hairdresser where I got pretty handy in a few days.'

> Having added barbering to his skills, Larry was told to make his own way to Yorkshire for the grouse-shooting.

'I started off for Yorkshire Moors on August 4 which was on Sunday and was at Bowes Moors on Saturday following. I went on feet the whole way.'

> He had covered some two hundred and thirty miles in seven days. His master, who presumably travelled more comfortably, joined him at the inn the next morning.

'There were a deal of lords' and squires' keepers there all which made the height of game of my master for bringing me from Ireland to shoot on the moors and I was a stranger and had nothing to say to those great men for a long time. I told any of them that liked to back their minds upon such a thing . . . I should bet a pound that my master and I would bring in more game from our gun than any other sportsman in the house, [but] they would not bet.'

> Just as well, as it proved, for on the glorious twelfth they acquired a 'big-headed' Yorkshire guide who led them for several hours on a fruitless search for grouse to the east of the moors and finally brought them within range of the guns of the other gentlemen where their dog, General, received '4 or 5 grains of shot full broad-side'.
>
> Two days later Lloyd abandoned the Yorkshire Moors and travelled north to Scotland. Larry and the dogs walked, by stages, to Leith. From there master, man and dogs took the packet steamer to Wick. The uncomfortable journey goaded Lloyd to a display of bad temper for which, in time, he became renowned. This particular outburst was observed by a silent onlooker and later reported in the edition of *Blackwood's Magazine* for July 1830. There is a long review of Lloyd's first book *Field Sports of the North of Europe* and then an unexpected postscript added by the anonymous reviewer –

'By the by, we remember meeting him a good many years ago, on board a Wick packet. He was somewhat seasick; and being enveloped in a monstrous dread-nought [heavy overcoat], he was not unlike a bear. Seasickness makes a man surly; and our author had nearly devoured a worthy friend of ours, who chanced to tread upon his toes as he lay upon a coil of cable. Under exasperation, he had a most formidable aspect and his growl was fearsome. We heard some talk about throwing somebody into the sea; but we came forward in our character of peacemaker, and with our crutch stopt the conflict . . .'

> This opinion of Lloyd was confirmed by the Swedish courtier F. von Dardel who illustrated two of his books. He considered that Lloyd was 'a really disagreeable type – the man besides being inconsiderate, lacks tact'.
> At Wick, Llewellyn Lloyd and Larry made their way to the house of the local laird, a Mr Sinclair.

'. . . away to the moors we went with General and Mellow, a setter dog . . . My master was like a good many sportsmen, he wanted to go all over the whole of the mountains at the one time. We paced up a hill very thickly covered with heath and left the game and craggy ground behind us. We hunted for two hours and a half and got two shots at a brace of old barren birds . . . just at the house we found birds which led us to plenty of game in so much ease. We had twenty or thirty brace of grouse in view at one time . . . My master shot well . . .'

> For the next month they shot over the moors of Caithness and Banville began to find Lloyd a hard taskmaster.

'Saturday 7 of September
This morning I was up at half past 5 o'clock. I got all things ready for my master then had to dress his hair, feed my dogs and saddle the pony, and hardly had time to taste a bite for my breakfast . . . only a small piece that I took in my hand. Then we shot over the same ground as we did last Thursday. The birds was wild and my master was very cross with me this night. In all the game was 27 grouse, 1 snipe – 28 [head].

Monday 9 of September
This was a hard day on both man and dog. It rained and blew – we hunted all the dogs. The birds very wild and he shot pretty well, killed 27 grouse and 2 snipes, 1 hare – 30 [head]. I was up at 5½ o'clock and went to my bed at 11½ o'clock. I dressed my master's hair before I took my wet things off and after all I cannot please him.'

> Hard-driven by his master all week, the Catholic Irishman found himself harassed by Scottish Protestants on Sundays.

'This day I was within doors the most of it for, as the old saying is, that

Larry records how Llewellyn Lloyd dressed in 'Scotch clothes' when out shooting in the Highlands.

anyone is hard worked all the week he will not run about much on the Sabbath day . . .

All the people there was going to make me go to the kirk with a white sheet on my shoulders to ask their forgiveness, but they did not persuade [me] in it.'

At the end of one hard day's shooting –

'We arrived rather late at a farm house, the gentleman's name was John McKinley, a drover of cattle to England some years ago . . . the master of the house was in the parlour in company with my master . . . I was called into the parlour to get a glass of toddy, which I wanted it bad for it was a hard day on me. The master of the house asked me if I was a Catholic, to which my answer was "yes", and he said that all the Irishmen that died in the faith was in hell . . . My master said "What do you think of that?" I said that was well for all Scotchmen, for hell was full by this time, and taking my glass in my hand [I was] wishing them good night. In this man's house I was forced to sleep in an outhouse that there were neither door nor window. My dogs slept in the kitchen for it was too cold for them to sleep with me. I covered myself with hay, and in the morning was all covered with a white robe for it snowed in the night.'

Larry fed the dogs on oatmeal and milk and his own diet was not much richer, oatmeal bread and 'starbast' with milk, though he could sometimes supplement this with trout and rabbits that he caught and cooked for himself and his master. Lloyd could not bear to miss a day's shooting and was out in all weathers. This fell hard on Larry, especially as his master could only afford one pony between the two of them.

'Wednesday 11 of September 1822
This morning I was up at 5 o'clock and indeed I was very happy . . . to get out of my bed as it was so cold that I hardly could get a wink of sleep. We started off at 7 o'clock and it was blowing and raining so fast that we hardly could stand on our legs. We faced to the north and we crossed a river above a large lake . . . The birds were as wild as hawks. They are always the same in stormy weather. We walked for above 7 hours and did only kill 7 grouse. I saw a poor little family in a little wretched hovel where the children was almost naked . . . I was wet the whole day to the skin and it is not a good thing for man or dogs to be out in such weather.

Thursday 12 of September
We shot the whole day until it was dark, then my master mounted the pony and I behind him for some time, then dismounted and he left Poor Larry and the dogs to make the best of their way to Thurso where I arrived at about 12 o'clock and I was obliged to carry the dog Carlo on my back above a mile, he was so knocked up that he would not follow.'

In mid-September Llewellyn Lloyd planned an expedition to the Orkneys.

'Wednesday 18 of September
This morning I was delighted to see the sea so smooth as we were going across it to the Orkney Islands. I got all things ready for starting off. I put all on board. At 12 o'clock there were a lady to come in the boat, but did not think it proper to come . . . with four men in the boat. I was sick, master the same, the dogs shared the same fate.

Mr Heddle was the gentleman's name that my master went to see. He had a fine lady for his wife, they had eight or ten women servants and one little boy. The women was very dirty indeed, for they would leave anything undressed until it would stink, for at one time I plucked eight or ten snipes of the finest I ever saw and they never dressed them, which was a great pity. I often was hard set to get a drop of milk for my poor dogs, and all of them would be sitting all around.'

> They spent just over a week in the Orkneys and, according to Banville, it rained every day. The shooting was not good and the fleas were troublesome, making no distinction between man and master.

'This morning I was up at an early hour and I was very happy to get rid of the black troop. I mean the fleas, for they were in thousands in the bed that I lay in. I went and found my master with his clothes on, for he was so tormented with the same he could not sleep . . .

After breakfast we started off to shoot. We saw a great quantity of snipes [but] my master hardly gave himself time to shoot at one of them. We hunted over five dogs and they were very good ones, but the mountains was all too bare in cover . . . as the heather was burned some years ago and the frost do take good care not to let it get up ever since . . . In the course of the day I saw where a giant's cave was. It was cut into a large rock that was lying in a deep valley. It had two pillows left in the rock for them to lay their heads on to the north and in the side of the cave to the west there were a large place cut out of the rock as it was for the wife when bearing with child. The stone which they suppose they used to stop up the door I think eight or ten men would be hard set to stir it . . . I went and lay down in it and also left them a powder canister to drink out of when they would come that way.

At the south side of it there is a very high mountain, and this guide told me that there were hundreds of eagles in it. There is holes in the rocks for near five or six hundred feet high and the Large Eagle sleeps and breeds there and do always feed before sunrise or after sunset unless the days is wet and stormy . . . and then they will come out in the middle of the day and bawl like cats all over the tops of the mountains . . . [The guide said that] he tried it both to keep foxes and goats but all to no use . . . no foxes for the eagles would eat them all and no goats, the rocks too steep for them.'

> On Monday 23 September they made the crossing to Kirkwall with Lloyd in typical ill-humour.

[25]

'The wind was from the eastward and blowing a stiff gale and all the family thought to prevail on my master not to go that morning . . . Then my master was so angry [with] me that he seemed as if he was mad and got his breakfast, but I got none, which was often the case with those days. We started down to the boat and it was raining fast. I had nothing on but my shooting coat and there did a clergyman come down to see us off and as luck would have it he brought his cloak, and when he saw me going in to the boat and sitting down and the wind and waves coming on me, his heart felt for me, he offered me his cloak and said he would go home without it which my master took it and I got his . . . [This parson] also told me that he would take me for his man if I would like to stop with him after my master was done sporting in that part, which was a good offer, but I would not have it as my master always said that he would get me a good place one day or the other.'

> Banville found the town of Kirkwall 'one of the dirtiest that I ever saw in all my life', also over-populated with women 'about eight or ten to the one man'. The east wind brought more rain and hailstorms so that the local guides refused to come out shooting with them. Lloyd was undeterred, but on the 26th they returned to Mr Heddle's house on the Island of Hoy and sailed the following day for the mainland.

'This morning I got up and got all things ready for my master and then dressed his nob . . . I then fed my dogs, but that was a bad thing for when we went to sea they were all sick. I and my master was the same. The wind was in the same point as yesterday, blowing a good gale. The boat used to fill up with water up to our knees and master was obliged to bale it out in his turn. The poor dogs that was round me used to throw up in turn – I looked like one that was dead.'

> From their landing-place they made their way across land to Thurso, shooting as they went.

'My master and I rode off on a grey pony. He was dressed with Scotch clothes and I was in my green shooting clothes which made all that saw us stare at us. We came to our old ground where we found plenty of birds . . . My master shot well. We left off shooting at the close of the night. My master rode around a road and I went across the moor with my dogs and gun . . . The night was very dark [but] I travelled home quite happy with my dogs and gun. I came just into town at 11 o'clock and went to my bed at half past 12. In this town there do a piper and drummer go round every morning at 4 o'clock which I found a great service to me during my stay in the town.'

During the weeks that followed Lloyd's frequent outbursts of bad temper made life very hard for Larry.

'My master was forced to put on wet stockings this day, for the maids did not wash or dry them on the Sabbath day which he would not let me ride behind him to spite me on that account.

Monday 7 of October 1822

I was up early for I was willing to have all things ready for my master's coming . . . The mistress of the house did not give me my breakfast but was waiting for my master's arrival, but when he came he was very angry with me to think that I had not got my breakfast before that time of day. It was raining so fast that they all thought that no-one but a madman would go out shooting. It was ten to one fitter to be in the house at home by the fireside than to be on the moors. The whole country was wet near ankle-deep. The game was wild as kites. He shot well, bagged 25 grouse . . . We had a guide out with us, but he did not like to wade through a large river . . .

Tuesday 8 of October

. . . This was a hard day's work on me. I hardly rode this day a quarter of a mile and my honoured master was so angry with me that he swore at me so much that the man that was with us swore that he would not go with such a mad-brained man as he was if he would give half what he was worth to him . . . I was home after dark, had to clean all things and never changed my wet clothes and went to my bed at 12 o'clock.

Wednesday 9 of October

I was up at 5 o'clock and got all things ready for my master to go to Achavanich. Then I found that the saddle hurted the pony's back which made my master swear at me and also swore that he would make me carry all the game that he would shoot in the course of the day in a basket on my poor back . . . I was to start off with it on my back and it weighed about twelve or fourteen pounds. I had at the same time sixteen or seventeen pounds of shot and two or three pounds of powder on my back, and all the people that was in the town was looking at me . . . If I was in my own country I should not do any such thing for his honour or any other on this earth, but I carried it two or three miles from the house and then his passion abated and he sent a boy back with the basket. I carried all the game home and was in at a late hour and had to do all things. I went to my bed at half past 11 o'clock, tired enough.

Saturday 12 of October 1822
We shot across the hills to Achavanich where we found only a few birds. They were as wild as hawks and would not let us get a shot at them and it made my master so mad that he swore at me and said that he would send me home in a herring boat. I told him to do it as soon as he liked and that I would write to my friends and let them know how he was treating me in this country. He did not [say] any more to me for near one hour, then he called me to him and put his hand into his pocket and gave me one pound to spend, which it was a good thing for me. He do sometimes be in such a temper that it would make anyone hate the ground that he would walk on. I done everything that do lay in my power for him since I came to this part and I believe that he would give me one of his shirts off his back if I wanted it.'

For a short time after this Lloyd's temper improved, and the following Monday Banville reports –

'My master shot well and the dogs behaved well and what was more pleasure to me was my master was in a good mind all day. We travelled hard all day and it was no trouble to me to do so when my master was in a good mind as when master and man is in the harmony of chatting about the sport of the field nothing is too hard for either of them.'

However things soon reverted to normal.

'This whole day I was cleaning and after all I am not able to please my ill-tempered master. Part of the time I was wishing to be in my own country where I could go to my own chapel . . . My master is never satisfied with me on Sunday – what do be the reason I cannot tell . . .

Since I came to this country with him I never saw any man that changed so much, and I am sorry to say it is for the worse. The devil himself cannot put up with him sometimes.'

They returned to Mr Sinclair's house at Lybster for a time and Larry had further worries there, for the dogs all contracted mange which, he said, was common in both men and dogs in that part of the country. By this time it was November and Lloyd knew that he would soon have to leave Scotland. Before he went, however, he was determined to take part in a seal-hunt.

'Thursday 7 November

This was a fine day with the wind from the north, which was in favour of my master's wishes to go after the seals. I do not say but I myself have a wish to see it too, as I hear a deal of talk about it.

Friday 8 of November

This was as fine morning as anyone ever saw. We all got ready after breakfast to go to the seals' cavern . . . My master shot several balls at my hat forty or fifty yards from him which he made good shots at . . . I amused them all hitting small stones of the beach when I threw them up.

Then we all got into the boat. There were ten or twelve men and we were all armed with a thick stick for to hit the seals as they would run for the water as it is their only safety, for nothing can hurt them when they get into it. Our boat was a large one and we got into three of them and it was a fine sight to see . . . the rocks all dripping with water. Although the rocks were two or three hundred feet in height the sound or hollowing of the waves was most beautiful to the hearing. We went into them with one man with twelve or more candles in his hands, all lit to show us some light as it was quite dark. The seals all run for the water and each man stopped them with a light nap on the nose. I was dragged into the boat with a seal by the forepaw or fin . . .

We all thought to go into the large cave or cavity in the rocks with the boat, but it stuck in the upper part of the cave with the swell of the sea which put all the men into a fright. All of them threw their weight on the boat at the swell of the billow, then all of them held on to the anchor . . . it was a large stone that they let down at the entrance to the cave.

They set off home again for a smaller boat and left me on the rocks . . . I lay down and slept very sound. I was wet from the toe to the top of my head, but I do not remember ever getting an hour's rest that done me more good in my life.

At their return they would not take me in the boat as the old men said that there was not room for me.

My master gave me his gun to shoot at some of them if I could, I got two shots but to no use. I have seen ten or twelve of them at one time with their heads out of the water, but they would not keep it hardly while a man could take up his gun. After the space of near one hour they came out to me with the glad tidings that they killed a few of them . . . All that was killed that day was 19 head . . .

After dinner my master went to two or three caves to see if he could kill any of them as he was fond of the sport, but I stopped at home, which I think was the best place for me. I believe that there was no one into those caves for a great many years before and I think that it will be the same from this time forward as the old men did not like the same at all.'

Lloyd prepared to return to London, but, reluctant to leave his sport, he stole one last day's shooting.

'This morning I got up at an early hour and hardly had a bit of a shoe to my foot . . . My right foot was very bad with a pain that seized it a few days ago. I went off after breakfast and I could not walk at all. We had a good frost on the moors which I put my foot into water that had good thick ice on it, after that I took off both of my shoes and threw them both into a stream of water there, to never call for them again.

I walked all day without any shoes and was as well in both mind and health as if I could walk with the finest of shoes or boots. This day it was both wet and stormy and the birds was as wild as hawks. It was not fit to have anything out, either dog or man. When I came home wet through, my master made me go into the parlour to show the ladies my poor naked toes that was among the heather all day which were after making their appearance through my stockings. I then went and put a few curls into my master's hair. I was rather tired . . . My master is to start by the coach in the morning if all do be well which I am not the least sorry for it as my dogs and myself is quite tired of it.

Tuesday 12 of November 1822
This morning I was up at a little after 4 o'clock, packed up all the game for my master to take with him to London as he was forced away by the coach at half past 6 o'clock. He left me in the middle of strangers with five mangey dogs as bad as ever I saw in all my life.'

By devoted nursing Larry coaxed his dogs back to health and took them out for a final day's shooting with Mr Sinclair.

'They behaved well, [but] he shot so bad it was enough to make me hate the day that Mr Lloyd left the country, [for] although it was trouble it was pleasure to see him knock them down right and left, but that was not the case with this gentleman.'

The following day, 29 November, Banville took ship for England.

[30]

'We were tossed about until the Friday following not knowing what moment
would be the last with us all. I did not eat hardly anything, but I drank a
deal of coffee and tea. The mate of the vessel was very civil to me and [so
were] all the men, [but] the Captain often said that he would throw me
overboard, for it was on my account that they had such a bad passage . . .

We were on the way nineteen days. I lost one dog out of five which his
name was Cato, the finest hunter dog that I saw this long time. I landed at
Woolwich and put all my boxes into a house at Essex side of the river and
walked home to Leytonstone, with my four dogs scarce able to walk and
myself was the same.

At my arrival they were quite surprised as they all thought that I was
lost, dogs and vessel, as there was no account of us for so long a time . . . At
night my master came home and swore and cursed that it was my fault of
the dog to die. But how could I keep him alive? Poor Mellow was so bad
with a swelled throat . . . and he did say that I took no care of them and he
would rather to hear of my dying than the dog. I thought it was rather hard
for him to say so to me after I travelled with him for so long a time, and I
am well aware that the reader will see that I done all that was in my power
to do.'

There follows a gap of nine months in Banville's daily account of
his life. It seems probable that he spent that time in the Lloyd
household at Leytonstone. There he seems to have found a kindred
spirit in Llewellyn Lloyd's mother, for she was later described by
one of the Hoare family as 'Larry's great friend, she is a most nice
old lady and though a friend [a Quaker], describes bear shooting
with the greatest glee . . .'

By 1823, however, Lloyd had evidently kept his promise to find
Larry a good position in England. His new master was to be a
distant relative of Lloyd's, Thomas Fowell Buxton.

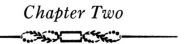

Chapter Two

THOMAS FOWELL
BUXTON

1823–24

Larry says that his first sight of Mr Buxton was in the House of Commons. He saw a man of thirty-seven years, over six foot in height, and of a grave and scholarly appearance. He was active and a keen sportsman, but he had nearly died of a 'bilious fever' in 1813 and his health was not robust.

In 1823 Buxton was the Whig Member of Parliament for Weymouth. He was deeply involved in the movement for prison reform and had already published *An Inquiry whether Crime and Misery are produced or prevented by our present system of Prison Discipline*. He was widely regarded as the natural successor to William Wilberforce as the leader of the campaign for the abolition of slavery.

The Buxtons came from Essex, and Thomas Fowell's father had been High Sheriff of the county, but he had died in 1792 leaving his six-year-old son as nominal head of the family. Thereafter he was deeply influenced by his mother, a member of the Society of Friends, later described by her son as 'a woman of very vigorous mind . . . large-minded about everything . . . fearless . . . ardent and resolute'. She did not force her religion on her children [Buxton remained all his life a member of the Church of England], but her Quaker morality dominated their childhood. They were allowed 'little indulgence, but much liberty'. After some early schooling with Dr Charles Burney at Greenwich, Thomas Fowell was sent

---

The crowded decks of a steam packet did little to help overcome the effects of sea-sickness.

Seals. 'At night after dinner my master went to two or three caves to see if he could kill any of them as he was fond of the sport . . .'

Engraved by G.Hunt.

to Trinity College, Dublin, for he had expectations of inheriting property in Ireland. He studied there from 1803–7 and took many prizes.

As a young man Buxton became friendly with the Gurney family of Earlham Hall outside Norwich. His particular friend was John Gurney, but there were also seven sisters and three brothers, attractive, intelligent and much influenced by their Quaker father. Elizabeth, one of the older girls, married Joseph Fry and dedicated her life to prison reform. Thomas Fowell fell in love with Hannah, the fifth daughter, and they were married in May 1807. Louisa, said to be the liveliest of them all, married Samuel Hoare.

The following year, his Irish expectations having come to nothing, Buxton entered the family brewing business of Truman, Hanbury and Co. where he carried out a complete reform of the administration. He also provided his workmen with a schoolmaster and threatened to dismiss all who had not learned to read and write within six months. Although deeply interested in the political and religious issues of the day, especially prison reform and slavery, it was not until 1817 that Buxton accepted a Parliamentary candidacy, being returned as MP for Weymouth the following year. He proved a powerful speaker in the Commons and worked tirelessly for his chosen causes.

Buxton's marriage to Hannah Gurney was a very happy one and between 1807 and 1823 eleven children were born: Priscilla, Thomas Fowell I, Susannah, Edward North, Hannah, Rachel, Louisa, John Henry [Harry], Richenda, Thomas Fowell II and Charles. However, when Banville joined the family there were only six children still living. Susannah had died as a baby in 1811, and then, in the space of five terrible weeks in 1820, four of the other children died. Thomas Fowell, the eldest son, was sent home from school with an unnamed fever and died within a few days. Then the three little girls, Hannah, Rachel and Louisa contracted measles on top of whooping cough and also died within a few days of each other. 'Thus, in little more than a month', wrote Buxton in his journal, 'have we lost the darlings and delights of our life; but they are in peace.'

It was after the tragic events of 1820 that the Buxtons came to spend their leisure times in Hannah's native county of Norfolk. The Buxton Game Books, which survive for these years, show that

'Sir Thomas Fowell Buxton, MP, 1786–1845' by George Richmond.

A page from the Game Books kept jointly by the Buxtons and the Hoares. The memoranda are in several hands; in this case the writing appears to be that of Sam Hoare junior and dates from 1828. It is notable that partridges were so much more numerous than pheasants.

Buxtons, Gurneys and Hoares had already been in the habit of shooting in the Cromer area at week-ends for some years, recording their bags with dedication and competitive enthusiasm. By 1823 the Buxtons had acquired the lease of Cromer Hall from the Wyndhams. Hannah's sister Louisa and her husband Sam Hoare were sharing the house with them, but were soon to purchase Cliff House not far away. Both families had houses in Hampstead which they occupied during Parliamentary sessions, but they always tried to spend the autumn in Norfolk where the brothers-in-law shared the shooting at Cromer and on the estates of the widowed Mrs Upcher of Sheringham Hall.

Banville, the new Irish servant, was soon sent off to Norfolk to make himself useful.

'Thursday 28 of August 1823

This day I went in to London where I saw T. F. Buxton Esq., MP, who asked me if I ever drove a gig and horse, which I told his honour I did, which it was the truth. Four days he allowed me to go 126 miles and take a grey mare and four dogs and a fishing net . . . I got up at an early hour and I started off and travelled with much pleasure to myself the whole journey to Cromer where I arrived about 5 o'clock on Sunday 31 of August 1823.'

> The Cromer that Banville came to in 1823 was scarcely more than a large fishing village on the bracing north-east Norfolk coast. It had a fine church, a lighthouse and a lifeboat station. There were some good houses, but most were small and the streets were narrow and badly paved. The fishermen and their vessels were picturesque

Old Cromer Hall, leased by the Buxtons in 1820. In 1828 George Wyndham, the owner, moved in and began to renovate and improve the property, but no sooner was it completed than it was destroyed by fire. The present Cromer Hall was then built on the same site.

[35]

A view of Cromer showing the church and the lighthouse.

to visitors, but no doubt there was also a pervasive odour of salt, tar and fish. Improvements were coming fast, however, for Cromer was beginning to enjoy a period of considerable popularity as a bathing-place for gentlefolk in the warm summer months. There was talk of resurfacing the roads with macadam. A school for girls was about to be opened to match the existing one for boys. Many well-to-do families acquired property in the town. Cromer, in fact, was becoming quietly fashionable.

What did Larry make of this new situation? Unfortunately his first impressions of Norfolk are somewhat garbled, perhaps reflecting his bewilderment or possibly his lack of spare time for writing up his journal.

'Monday 1 of September 1823
This morning I got up at early hour and watered my mare, and fed my dogs, and washed the cab. Then they put me to cut sticks and to lay straw . . .

and to mow grass. All those things I done and the pony that they put to this cab run away with it and broke it. It was sent to Norwich. I thought them all very queer people in this part of the country.

Tuesday 2 of September

This morning I got up at early hour, started off in the phaeton with my master and took those two dogs with me to shoot at a gentleman's place of the name Fakenham. We took up a young gentleman with us of the name of Harry Upcher [Mrs. Upcher's eldest son] at a lodge of Sheringham. Then we went on to a place of the name of Holt where we changed horses and drove off to the above-mentioned place where my master got his breakfast, but I got nothing to eat or drink. My master rode a black shooting pony and I walked. The fields was a mile across them and the two dogs that I had were strangers to me and I to them, and my master wanted to shoot and would not give me time to say a word to the dogs, or to do anything but run after him from one part to the other. The dogs would not drop to the birds or to the gun; all was against me. It put me in mind of fox-hunting more than partridge-shooting. We got our dinner, and after dark we set off and my master and Mr. Upcher went asleep on the way home . . .

I spoke about how they used me at my coming to this part of the world. They used me so that my hands and fingers was blistered so that I hardly held a knife or fork, but my heart was in its right place. One used to come to me and ask me what I was, and then that one would go away and another used to come, so that they made me quite sick of them, but I used to say only very little which is the best way for any stranger to do. I stopped with them for a few days and done everything that I could with great spirits.

I then was sent to Sheringham to a keeper's house of the name of Will Steward, a good-natured fellow, but his wife was one of the greatest brawlers I ever met with. I used to go out shooting every day and out watching by night which was rather hard on me. We used mostly to go to kill rabbits every night which keeped us all in good spirits. I stopped in Sheringham from September until June 27 1824 and during the said time I was at the killing of 1,717 rabbits.'

There were stirring events in Cromer that autumn had Banville had the time and inclination to record them. On 10 September 1823, the *Norwich Mercury* reported that Cromer

'presented an unusually animated scene on Wednesday last, occasioned by the influx of gay company to witness the exercising of the Cromer and Mundesley life-boats, and the experiment of conveying assistance to stranded vessels. The unclouded beauty of a delightful autumnal day encouraged many parties from a considerable distance, to repair to this part of the coast, and amongst the gay assemblage we recognised members of most of the principal families of the neighbourhood . . .'

Five members of the Mundesley life-boat crew were successfully 'rescued' by the use of the mortar gun from a boat moored three hundred yards out to sea, and the Cromer boat 'performed some evolutions in a beautiful manner'. The rival claims of Captain Manby's ingenious mortar gun and an improved version devised by Mr Haze, an engineer from Saxthorpe, were then comprehensively put to the test and the Haze gun, sponsored by Hannah Buxton's cousin, Miss Anna Gurney, proved superior in all respects. Finally there was a rowing match between the two life-boats, the Cromer boat emerging victorious. Fireworks were set off from the jetty and the only popular regret seems to have been the absence of a dance for the young people to round off the day.

By the end of the following month the holiday-makers had departed from Cromer and the sea front presented a bleaker and more threatening aspect. On 31 October the *Duchess of Cumberland*, a collier brig, ran upon the rocks off the Cromer lighthouse. It proved impossible to launch the life-boat and the mortar guns failed to reach the vessel. After four hours of fruitless effort the ship broke up and there seemed no hope of saving the captain and his crew from drowning. The local paper records that many gentlemen were present, including Mr Buxton and Sam Hoare's eldest son. Charles Buxton, in his Memoir of his father, writes that Mr Buxton actually saved the life of one of the crew by diving into the sea without a rope and holding him 'against the strong drawback of the retiring billow' until others could drag them back to shore. 'The deed was considered by those on shore to have been one of extreme peril and daring.'

This wreck, and others like it that autumn, led to the formation of the Association for Saving the Lives of Shipwrecked Mariners, headed by Lord Suffield and Colonel Wodehouse. The Buxtons and Hoares were regular subscribers.

Unfortunately there is no daily account of this period in Banville's diary, but it seems that towards the end of his first nine months in Norfolk, Llewellyn Lloyd asked for Banville's services on another sporting expedition, this time to Sweden. Larry agreed to go, but there were at least two people in Norfolk who were sorry to see him leave.

'Mrs Upcher, the lady of the manor, seemed very sorry for me going away. She gave me 10s. on my master's account and I payed every one that I owed anything to and started off a fresh fellow with the good wishes of most of the neighbours. I left a young girl behind me which I think will be mine if I ever come to the county again. Mrs Upcher gave me a Bible to take with me which I left with the young woman who have my heart. Also Mrs Upcher told me that I was with a good master who had plenty of money and that I was going away to face the seas and travel with a man that had none, but all that I did not mind. Go I did.

I must say a few words with my simple pen about my master who I am about to leave behind me . . . He asked me if I owed anything in Sheringham and said that he would gladly pay it, which I thanked his honour for it, but I took good care not to go beyond my money as I did not know what day I should leave his service, as all servants ought to think a gentleman's place of service is no estate, for one day he may please and the other may be discharged, as it is often the case. He gave me great credit for going with Mr Lloyd as he said I was one out of a thousand, and that he would take care to take me into his service again at my return to this country. Of course I was very much obliged to his honour for the offer, but I could not tell whether I should be fit for service at my return. He then made me a present of £5 which was a great thing for a gentleman to do with a servant who was going away.

"Good-bye" he said, "and I shall be happy to see you again as my servant."'

Chapter Three

SWEDEN

1824–25

Llewellyn Lloyd had visited Sweden for the first time in 1819. He had been immensely attracted by its opportunities for hunting and fishing and, in consequence, he had now arranged to rent part of a peasant's house in Värmland for use as a base during his sporting expeditions.

A few weeks were spent at Lloyd's house at Leytonstone while they prepared for their forthcoming trip. Unfortunately, Lloyd's sudden irritabilities which had been such a prominent feature of their Scottish expedition again soured their relationship. However, at this early stage of their renewed contact, Larry did not take it too much to heart.

'I think it was the 16th of July that we left London. I went down in a boat under one bridge of London. I went and asked all the people there where the boat was going to and some told me if I would go down to Gravesend I would find her. I did so, but did not find it to be the case and I was forced to come back again and slept at an inn on shore that night. Then went to the foreman's office in the morning where they soon told me where to find her. My master was aboard and he stopped and swore at me and said he thought I had run away, which my answer was that he had known me long enough [not] to be afraid of my running away. He then drew his passion in and he was in good

---

A watercolour of Cromer beach painted by Robert Dixon in the early 19th century. Cromer was a favourite subject for the Norwich School group of painters, and this went hand-in-hand with the growth in popularity of the town as a watering place.

Yarmouth Quay, painted in 1823 by George Vincent, was a busy port for coastal traffic and ships from the Baltic. It was a frequent point of disembarkation by Larry.

Overleaf: Map of the Cromer area made by Frank Pank, a neighbour of Banville's when he first came to Norfolk

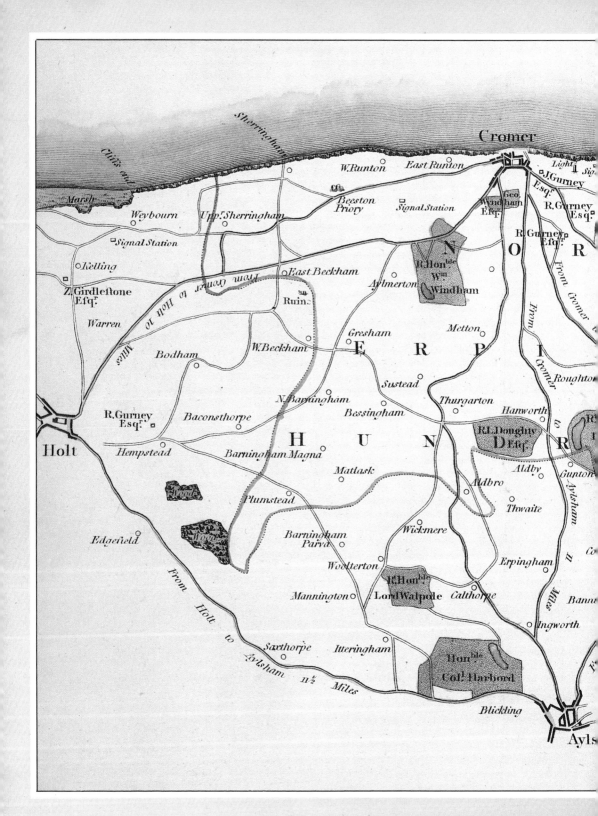

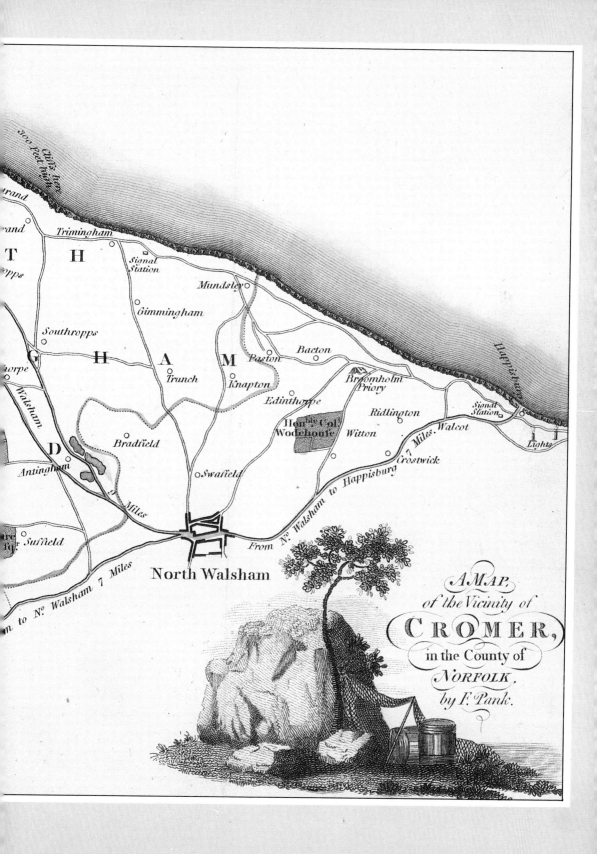

Chalk Cliffs 300 Feet high

Strand

T

H

Trimingham

Signal Station

Mundsley

Gimmingham

Southropps

opps

pps

G

H

A

M

Paston

Bacton

Trunch

Knapton

Broomholm Priory

horpe

Walsham

Edinthorpe

Ridlington

Signal Station

D

Hon.ble Col. Woodhouse

Witton

Walcot

Lights

Bradfield

Antingham

7 Miles

Crostwick

Swaffield

3 Miles

From N.º Walsham to Happisburg

Happisburg

re

ly: Suffield

n to N.º Walsham 7 Miles

North Walsham

A MAP,
of the Vicinity of
CROMER,
in the County of
NORFOLK.
by F. Pank.

friends with me. In a few minutes we were all as good as master and man could be. I went ashore at Gravesend where I bought some brushes to clean his boots and shine them.'

No accommodation was provided on the ship for Larry.

'I went aboard the vessel or brig and never took off my clothes or lay on a bed for nine days and nights. And my food – I need not say it was the best – but I was well pleased with it as I could get a herring when I wished for it with some potatoes. I fed my four dogs all the whole way with a bit of dry biscuits and water. They did well . . . The whole time we were on the water I used to be so sick as not able to put one foot before the other.

A young Swedish woman used to come on the deck and joke with all the sailors and passengers and then used to go and tell my master that all were very unkind to her which if she was anything like a decent girl, no one would say anything to her. One day she was on the deck and I was roasting a herring for myself and a spark went on to my pantaloons and burned a hole and she said "I will go and tell your master" and I said, "You may go and be damned for what I care for you or anyone of your sort". She ran immediately to him bawling, saying I abused her before all the sailors. My master was not well pleased, but did not say much to me about it.'

The ship sailed north within sight of the Dutch and Danish coasts and reached its destination on 26 July.

'We lay at anchor at the mouth of the river within five or six miles of Gothenburg. This day I saw the young prince coming down the river. We had the honour to give His Grace a cheer, three times three, which in return to it he uncovered his head which it was a cap he wore. A fine looking man was he.

This day the officers came on board and would not let us take our things on shore. We went up to town in the large boat belonging to the vessel and then my master was forced to come on board for his dress things as he was going to dine with the Prince.

In the course of the day I saw the King and Queen and the princesses also. Fine looking young women the latter were. The King was a fine looking war-like man.'

Charlotte Upcher, daughter of Lord Berners, painted by Richard Westall at Sheringham with the sea behind. She was married to Abbot Upcher in 1809 and widowed ten years later. They had three sons and three daughter. When Charlotte died in 1857, Hannah Buxton said shw was 'such a reigning person'.

This king, Charles XIV, was Bernadotte, Prince of Pontecorvo and once one of Napoleon's marshals. He had been invited to become heir to the Swedish throne when direct heirs were lacking and when the country needed a strong king, for Sweden had become involved in the turmoil of the Napoleonic wars.

Immediately upon leaving the ship, Llewellyn Lloyd and Larry Banville began their hunting and fishing. Lloyd published his impressions of this Swedish trip in his book *Field Sports of the North of Europe*. Further books were published by him describing his hunting experiences in Scandinavia and peasant customs in Sweden. Larry, for his part, recorded his impressions in his diary.

'This morning we got a boat and a white-headed young man to take us up the river to a place of the name of Headed. The wind was against us. My master shot all along side of the river . . . He killed 15 snipe and 4 wild ducks. About half way, I saw 8 wild ducks close by a house where I thought them to belong to the house. He knocked down 2 of them.

The night was fast approaching and the wind had risen also. We put up my master's cloak for a sail which helped us well. After dark we saw a light, but to our sad disappointment we found we were near three miles from Headed. Our white-headed man scratched his hair and we set off again and not a drop of brandy with us. At last we got ashore and I carried my master out of the water for he was very ill.

He was after changing his shoes and stockings when we got on dry land. We were all both hungry and cold. My master, in one of his bad fits of temper, broke a bottle of brandy and spilled it all. He would gladly have accepted of some of it this night. When we were going up to the house we met with a small field of beans and was very well satisfied to eat some of them.

My master went to his bed as soon as he could get into bed. I waited on him. I then fed my dogs. Went to my bed at 12 o'clock in the same room with my master which I did not like at all. The night was dark.'

Each day's hunting was recorded in great detail by Larry who showed much interest in his new surroundings.

'Friday 13 of August 1824

This morning I went and got a great deal of small stones to throw into the likely parts of the river where it is thickly bedded with reeds as the ducks do

The rapids of Trollhättan. This part of the River Göta was a favourite fishing spot with
Llewellyn Lloyd and Larry, and one of them is shown playing a fish from the rocks. This
illustration appeared in Lloyd's book *Scandinavian Adventures*, published in 1854.

lie in them. My master shot well. It turned to very heavy wet and we had no
shelter whatever. My master sat down and I answered the same as an
umbrella. In the course of ten minutes I was wet through from my poor head
to my feet for the water was running down my back to the soles of my feet.

My master and Mr Harrison [Larry described him elsewhere as 'the
Consul'] got a boat and we went to cross the river to one of the finest reed-beds
that I ever saw in my life . . . We made the best of our way to the favourite
ground for the snipes. They were very wild, but by good shooting and
marking he bagged 24 snipe and 3 teal.'

The abundant lakes and streams meant that fishing was as popular
a sport as shooting.

'Thursday 9 September 1824
We went up the river – he to shoot and I to fish. He left me on a large rock
in the middle of the river for a long time. The waterfall here is one of the
finest in this part of the country. It is about 40 or 50 yards wide. The water
is always white with the force of it going down at such a pace . . . Above

[43]

this fall of the river it is like a large lake. We killed 5 salmon before breakfast. In the course of the day we killed 9 more and 4 carp.

I stopped up this night till 11 o'clock. Then I went in to the garden and picked a deal of worms to be ready for the morning to fish. We got a deal of them. It is very surprising to think that the least noise would frighten them so that you would hardly get one out of ten of them so at first I hardly got any of them, but by a little time I would take them in style.'

Fishing continued right through the winter months.

'I saw two men cutting holes in the ice which is 2½ feet deep. They cut the holes with a square cheddle with four edges on it and they take the ice out of the holes with a wooden shovel. They will put the net into it and will shove it along a pole about 20 or 30 feet in length. They will get the rope and pull it along. Perhaps they will draw it 100 yards and 50 in breadth, but that is all dependent on the size of the net. While I stopped with them they drew one place and got a deal of fish. They were small ones – I believe about three thousand in all.'

> Every few days Banville and his master moved their lodgings in their constant search for new and better hunting grounds. They crossed and recrossed the countryside in the region of Lake Vanern and the area to the south-west of the lake. Travelling was often by coach or carriage, but on many occasions they walked from one lodging to the next, shooting as they went.

'This morning I went and packed up all the luggage and got my breakfast. The young mademoiselle gave me a waistcoat to wear of her own weaving and all the household was, by appearance, sorry to part with Poor Larry. Then we started off.

The first town was Vanersborg. The first thing that took my attention were three turkeys fighting; the next was a man mending his carriage – it is so often the case in this country for they are often broken as the streets are so rough – and the next was a man cutting a window frame with his axe.'

> Banville was an interested sightseer and often set out on his own to look at unusual landscapes or to walk through the towns. However, rather than a general impression of the features of a place, it is usually details which reach the diary.

'After dinner I walked in to Gothenburg. The distance is about seven or eight miles. At the first of the town I saw a deal of people. They were all well dressed. They all were staring at me. There was a hearse in the middle of the people and the coachman was dressed with a blue cloth coat and a cocked hat and silver lace and white gloves and the whip was the finest I saw in Sweden. I stopped at the Consul's where I spent most of the evening writing a letter to send to my love in England.'

> During these months in Sweden, Larry kept up a regular correspondence with Sarah Lown, the girl he had been so sorry to leave behind in Norfolk. He 'bought two silver thimbles in hopes they will be given to S.L. by my own hand.'

'I saw a little of the town of Karlstad this day. It is a fine place. The streets is very wide and all paved with large stones and it is not very clean. They seem to be very civil people, at least they are to me at present. The girls took great delight in hearing me talk, but I was thinking of the girl I left behind me.'

> Larry was a most regular attender of Sunday services. Although a Roman Catholic, he showed no hesitation in taking part in Swedish Lutheran services.

'At my entering the Church it looked well for it was painted in all kinds of pictures and the ceiling was the same with the sign of the rainbow in it and a small ship hanging down and a thousand of spiders' webs in all parts.

There were a large gallery and, believe me, the men used to throw the spittles down on the floor so that it was enough to stifle me if the doors was not open or to drown young ducks, for if they would put their little foot into them they would never get them out again.

As for the clergyman, he was very handsomely dressed with a very nice vestment, very much like our clergymen in Ireland. The sign of the Cross was on one of the vestments and two letters that I know nothing about.'

> On several occasions Larry attended a village wedding service.

'Three couples was married . . . The young women were dressed very nice and they had a crown on each of their heads and was dressed like little girls with their necks all naked and their hair all hanging down to the full extent. When they came into the church the parson and one of the brides came in and four fiddles playing . . . As the service was done, the parson put on a rug and two young women and two young men held a shawl over them.'

> Lloyd and Larry spent Christmas at the house of Herman Falk, Mr Lloyd's near neighbour and friend. Falk was one of the most famous huntsmen in Swedish history. After early service in the

army and as a member of the Swedish parliament, he had been appointed Court Master of the Hunt in 1823. Llewellyn Lloyd received his training as a bear hunter from Falk and described in his books many exciting hunting expeditions shared by the two men.

Falk's house was a large one with a great number of servants and Larry noted their Christmas preparations with interest.

'I helped the girls in dipping candles. They all make twelve candles of a round and all of them fast at the bottom so they will go in one candlestick which looks well. They also make a cake with all kinds of the pictures of birds and fishes which they keep for the twelve days of Christmas which is a sure way of not being without bread . . .

This is belonging to the 23rd of the month of December – I mean St Thomas' Night – when I was fast asleep. I was awakened from my sleep and I beheld two young women approaching my bedside. One of them had a tray with coffee and biscuits. She was dressed with white and also twelve candles all lighting around her head and they were fastened on by a white handkerchief which made me at first think it very odd. The other young woman had a bottle of brandy and a glass which I had the honour of partaking some of them both . . .

Here is the way that they do take supper on the birthday of Our Lord and Saviour. They all have fish and groats and fat bacon – plenty of it. A few days before that day, the houses is all washed through and all the lower apartments strewed with cut straw, for what reason I cannot tell, but I should suppose that it is in remembrance of the Saviour coming to the world in a stable.'

Llewelyn Lloyd suffered from frequent bouts of illness and soon after Christmas became really ill.

'Monday 17 January 1825
This morning I waited on my master. He had a blister on his breast and he stopped at home all day . . . My master says he will go out shooting in the morning, but I would advise him to get well first.

Thursday 20
At 6 o'clock I took off the blister. Then after a little time, I lay down, but could not close my eyes with trouble and pains in my weary bones . . . He

told me that if anything happened to him he should leave a few lines in his writing case for me to say what he wished me to do.

Saturday 22

This day my master was very ill – all of it – although he got up and wrote a deal and said that he settled all his affairs. He asked me if I should like to spend my life in any one part of the world as he should send me where I liked as his friends would be most happy to do anything for him and also for me. He also paid me £2. 10. 0. that he owed me and all things he arranged as he thinks he is going to change lives. May it be a happy one! This day, I at one time thought I must shed some tears, but I did not for I thought it is no use to drop tears unless for my own sins.

This night I am going to sleep in the room next to his. This way I may be at his call if he will want me. I shall be most happy to strive to wait in all manner of things. I have made his bed this day twice and do all things the same as any maid.

Tuesday 25

Last night my master did not hardly close his eyes which is a bad sign. The doctor was to come, but he sent a letter and twelve powders – one of them to be taken every two hours.'

A week later Larry was writing –

'My master got worse this day. My master wrote a deal of letters to all his friends in England to inform them of his illness and begs of me to take care of my soul and not to have so much to think of when I am on my death bed. His feet are very cold and his throat is sore also. I put a poultice to his neck.'

However by the end of the following week, Larry was able to write –

'Friday 11 February

This was a fine day and my master went out, but is not well yet, but he is a deal better, of course. He have a cold and a cough.'

Then he adds, rather ruefully,

'I had a bad headache all day. My master said it was nothing.'

Usually Lloyd and Larry lodged in private houses. This meant that Larry mixed with the servants and often lived with them.

'I went to my bed of clean straw in the one room with a whole family of Swedes which there were eight in number besides myself. The room was so hot I got up and opened the door, but as soon as I was in the bed, the master of the house got up and shut it fast and said it was cold. My frame was tormented with the fleas for they were about me in some thousands and as for the flies they were about my face as much as to make me keep awake the whole night, which all made me wish for the daylight.'

And of another family, he wrote,

'The frau is in the bed very drunk. It is but little wonder for the house family is after drinking two kegs of brandy this eight or ten days and they will not think anything of drinking a full tankard of some brandy and then eat raw herrings after it. My master would kill me if I would drink a glass of it.'

The universal dirtiness of the people was repeatedly noted even in wealthy households.

'In all the dirty people that I ever saw, I think there is some of them in this part for they will make large heaps of their human dirt at the back parts of their little houses, so much, indeed, that a pig might be fattened on it.'

At a country house he complained that in his bed

'there is two or three thousand lice and the same number of fleas and the man that I sleep with in it, he really stinks above the earth.'

Larry found the Swedes' attitude to children somewhat disconcerting.

'This morning I got up at half past 5 o'clock and had to regret the treatment that a poor little child belonging to the man of the house got last night. It was all the night crying in the cradle, but no notice taken of it. No, no more than if it was not in the house at all. The mother of it took and tied it up all round the arms and legs with a kind of red cloth and it had the head out so it could bawl well which it did not forget to do . . .

I have seen a child about three or four years old drinking two glasses of brandy at supper which almost frightened me out of my wits . . .

Here is the way they give a small child a drink of milk. They have a small horn for the purpose, with a small bit of leather sewed to it and they will take some milk in their mouths and warm it and put it into the horn and then the child can drink of it.'

Larry often found himself the centre of attention for the local inhabitants.

'I went home as fast as I could and there did four of the better sort of men ride after me as fast as they could, but when they got past me, they gazed at me as long as they thought proper. Then they stopped at the inn and got so close to the door that I was obliged to force in the door between, which I thought it was rather rude of them. When I sat down to my dinner, there did two young women came in and stayed gazing at me the whole time I was at my dinner and which was a deal worse, they kept blowing their noses the whole time which made me tired of them two fair creatures.'

It is obvious that Banville was a popular figure with the Swedes.

'This night I sang some songs for the young mademoiselles and they sang in return and I believe we were both alike for I did not understand a word they said.

A deal of girls danced at a kind of party. They all got hold of each other by body and twisted round as fast as they could and a man in the middle of the ring making all manner of noise and all sort of forms which was a fine sight to see.'

Occasionally Larry would spend the evening in the company of his master and his master's friends.

'This night I amused several gentlemen in putting out a candle with my bear spear. I used to put the candle on the table on one side of the room and used to run across the room at it. The gentlemen tried, but could not make a good fist of it. My master could do it well.

Consul-general Wise told me that Lord Blomefield was to give me a bottle of Irish whiskey which it was very good of his Lordship to do. The gentleman was here and had a good many jokes with me.'

Larry's qualities as a servant were noticed with approval in the households where he and Mr Lloyd lodged.

'The lady of the house came to me at supper and asked me if I would like to stop with her when my master would leave for England, but my answer was "No"; and she said that I could have a wife there, but the maid was not my sort that I wished for a wife if she had a thousand pounds. And then they said to me that I might go out shooting almost every day if I would stop here and that they would behave well to me. That I make not the smallest doubt of as they are the best lady and gentlemen I met in this country whose goodness to me I shall never forget.'

> Llewellyn Lloyd's brother, Mark, now came to Sweden on a visit.
> He was held in high esteem by Larry.

'Sunday 13 March 1825

Mr Falk's brother came to me and said I was wanted below stairs. I went down and Mr Mark Lloyd was there. I really was so overjoyed to see him that I am not able to say what I felt.

We started off at 11 o'clock in two sledges – Mr Mark and I in one which was a pleasant journey for Poor Larry as this gentleman told me many a story on the way. The roads was very bad as most of it was through the woods and the snow very deep and no snow plough was worked in that neighbourhood. Then we got to our journey's end. I was as tired as my heart could wish for. I got their supper ready for them. Mr Mark knowing that I was not well, got my master's bed ready and helped me in everything and then got a hank of straw and shook it against the fire and lay on it himself. I went into a space like a small cupboard, just about four feet long and some thousands of fleas in it. I was up out of my short bed at 6 o'clock and thankful enough to be to get out of it. I got all things ready for the journey . . .

My master told me to lock up one of his trunks which it was always hard to be locked and when I did not turn the key, my master hit me in the face with his hand. Mr Mark cried shame on his dear brother. I ate a bit of bread at 2 o'clock and that was all that I ate the whole day. My master was so kind as to tell Mr Mark that I ought to be made to walk half the way.'

> More than anything else in Sweden, Larry looked forward to the
> prospect of a bear cull. At last the great day arrived.

'When we came to the place, there were between four and five hundred men. Mr Falk took great pains in putting them in order – twenty men under one man and all was obliged to stand face to face and all set off one deep which took up a great deal of the road. My master was complaining of his toes the most of the time. I had to rub his toes different times and wrap his shoes up in a rug and hay also to strive to keep them warm.

We were placed in the ring about 20 or 30 yards to have the first shots at the bear. I had a spear and a double gun and a rifle and two pistols and a spear that I should not be afraid of anything, but to our great surprise we heard a gun-shot at the further side of the ring. I said to my master, "There

A bear-hunt. Both the huntsman and his guide are travelling on skis and are accompanied by a hunting dog. The huntsman with his flat cap and checked trousers is Llewellyn Lloyd himself.

This triumphant procession back to the village shows the universal interest in bear-hunting. Lloyd, in his customary hunting jacket and checked trousers, can be seen beside the bear.

is the bear shot" . . . To our mortification we found it to be the bear that fell
to the shots. There were two men fired at him for it got one ball in at the
point of the shoulder and another in the back.

The poor men that was far from their home all disappeared their nearest
ways. I cannot tell what Mr Falk felt for he was in a great passion with the
men that shot the bear.'

> In spite of the occasional excitements of bear and wolf hunting,
> it was the constant hard work, his difficult master and general
> homesickness that led Larry to write rather wearily in May 1825 'I
> am tired of being here in this part of the world'.
>   However, within a week of this entry, Larry is packing his
> belongings and wondering if he will find all well when he reaches
> England. He left his master without a word of regret.

'Tuesday 17 May 1825
I started off at 6 o'clock. The morning was as fine as anyone could wish for.
About 9 o'clock I was obliged to stop on the road as one of the side traces
gave way . . . I saw a deal of wildfowl of all sorts. I also will say that I saw
37 swans on one lake. They were all belonging to the king. In the course of
the day's journey I lost 6 hours at different places. If any man wish to travel
fast in this country, let him send on a 'forward board' before him and the
horses will be ready at each stage for him.'

> On Friday he arrived in Gothenburg. He found lodgings for himself
> while he waited for a ship which would take him to England. He
> renewed his acquaintance with friends who took him on several
> outings.

'The three girls and I went into a boat and in the course of half a mile we
went under eight bridges and up the river. We arrived at 9 o'clock and took
breakfast with the family. The miss of the house showed me all parts of the
house and seemed well pleased that I went to see her. I was then taken into
the garden where it was all well laid out. Then the girls and myself went up
to the top of the hills, to cast my eyes all over the bare rocks of Sweden.'

> Other days were spent hunting mallard, snipe and landrail with
> the Consul and this period of waiting passed pleasantly.

'Wednesday 1 June 1825
This morning I was up at 5 o'clock and wished the Consul Harrison Esquire
and his maids "goodbye". They treated me in the same manner as if I was a

child of their own which I shall never forget it for their eyes was bathed in tears.

Thursday 2 June 1825

This was a wet morning and stiff gale. We stopped in the river the whole day. I was sick although it was fresh water which did surprise the Captain and all his men. This day I dined on a good piece of roast beef. I think it will be the last I shall eat until I land in old England.'

> After another day anchored in the river, the ship got under sail on Saturday.

'Sunday 5 June 1825

This morning the wind was in our favour. The Captain told me we ran 180 miles in twenty-four hours. The wind dropped which made me so ill I could not hold up my head.'

> The agony of sea sickness continued, so Larry's joy can be imagined when on Thursday –

'To my great happiness the Captain called me on the deck and said that I might go with him to Yarmouth. I got my things. Started off with the Captain and three men that was in the boat. We went to the Star Hotel and there I got a room and was happy to find that I was only about forty miles from Sheringham.

Friday 10 June 1825

This morning was fine. I went to the coach office and paid for my seat to Norwich and put my big coat on my seat. A large gentleman sat on it and I asked him for my coat or at least a part of it and he gave me a part of it and ne'er as much as opened his frog mouth. The stage where we changed horses at, he got off and I took the liberty of procuring the whole of my coat and let the silent gentleman sit on the bare board of the coach.

I arrived at Cromer at 8 o'clock and went up to the Hall. I was very happy to think that I was so near my young woman.'

> Larry was pleased by the warm reception he received from every-
> one. He had brought bird skins for the young boys at the Hall and
> plenty of good stories for his friends. He sums up his Swedish
> journeyings with the advice to his readers –

'Any gentleman that will go to Sweden to travel, let him not think that he will meet with everything to please his mind and if he will take a servant with him, he will not want one of the dandy sort.'

[53]

Chapter Four

MARRIAGE

1825–26

Banville returned to Sheringham to take up his life where he had left it nearly a year before. He made haste to seek out Sarah Lown, the girl who had been so often in his thoughts while he was away.

'Saturday 11 of June

I went and called at my love's father's and to my great joy she came herself and she went in with me into the parson's yard which I was not willing to go, but the family was all gone away . . . we stopped there for some time. I took a walk with my girl and I saw Mrs Upcher and two of her daughters, but did not speak to them. I came back and went in with her and asked them how they were and I found they were all well. I stopped up at Doughty's [the pub] until one o'clock.

Sunday 12 of June 1825

This morning I went up to see Mrs Upcher and all the ladies . . . and they seemed very happy to see me, and then her ladyship asked me to my dinner which I accepted of the offer, but to tell the truth I would rather let it alone. I called to see all the servants and all was happy to see Poor Larry again, but I was sorry to the heart to find that my worthy friend was gone to a better place I hope, William Steward was his name. We had a good dinner of beef and Norfolk dumplings.

After dinner I was obliged to go in to her room to speak to her . . . [She said] that I ought to speak about affairs to my supposed father-in-law and mother-in-law. But I told her that I should not say anything to them and that they were at their own pleasure to do what they liked and if it was not for herself [Sarah] I should not have returned to England, for the Consul would have taken me into his service. She told me that my master was to be my friend and to say nothing until his return from London. That was all that was worth notice that happened between us.'

The Lowns were a respectable family, tenants of Mrs Upcher. It is probable that Sarah's father was the carpenter, William Lown, to whom payment is made in the Overseers' Accounts of £1. 0. 0. for a coffin for Thomas Johnson in 1827. Both he and Sarah's brother, Leonard, served as Overseers of the Poor during the years between 1817 and 1827. They apparently had no objection to Sarah walking out with the young Irishman from the Hall and he soon became a regular week-end visitor.

'Saturday 18 of June

This day I got up at an early hour. After dinner I went to ferret with Edmund Lown [Sarah's other brother] . . . I went to walk in the evening with S.L. which was more to me than drinking tea with anyone in the world at present.

Sunday 19 of June

After church I went and had a pint of beer with a friend of mine, but I took tea with Mr Cranfield. Passing my girl's door I saw plenty of plum cake cut on a plate which I got a bit of it. At six o'clock it came to wet. It rise up a fine evening. We walked for a long time as the roads was good and dry . . .'

On Midsummer Day Larry took his sweetheart to Aldborough Fair.

'I dined at one o'clock, then Robert Doughty put to the cart and away we all started for the fair. The day was fine, the dust was flying all along the roads as we went. I saw a wagon going to the fair that held twenty-seven women and men. I spent the day in all kinds of amusement.

I went to see a show of people. There were a man that said that he was from the foreign parts – he had a ring of ivory out of the top of his nose, the same out of his both ears. I saw a girl of eighteen years and she was six feet five inches of height. Another was full as broad as she was long, another thirty-six inches high. They all three were well-formed women. My costs for the day was fifteen shillings.'

The next day orders came from Mr Buxton in London that Larry should go up to Cromer Hall to help the keeper, John Davison.

'Wednesday 22 of June

This morning I went to Cromer Hall where I was not welcome, I believe, by John Davison, but that makes little odds to me. I am ordered here by my master, T. F. Buxton Esq. M.P., and I have my living to seek by my hands, and of course I must strive to do it in a fair way with all that I meet with.

Monday 23 June
This day I spent it in a different way to what I ever spent one in this country
before. It was weeding barley. In the evening I went to see the other part of
the manor as I did like to see it, as I thought it was my duty to see all parts
of the ground that I should look over. I was wishing this day to hear from
my master L. Lloyd Esq. as I did not hear from him since I left him in
Stockholm.

Friday 27 of June
This was a misty morning. I went to my vermin traps in the Dole and found
a stoat in it. I came back by Burnt Hills where I got some strawberries for
the first time. I played cricket for a while, but I did not like the sport.'

At the end of July, Larry was sent on another journey. His destination was Gatehouse, and his purpose was to capture a quantity
of black grouse and bring them back to Norfolk for breeding. He
took the steam packet from Cromer to Leith, then the stage-coach
from Leith to Edinburgh where he bought 'two pairs of stockings
for 5s. 4d. which was very cheap in my mind'. From Edinburgh he
travelled in a heavily-laden coach into the mountains of Galloway,

'. . . the fairest hills that ever I passed before . . . green from the top to the
bottom, thousands of sheep and a shepherd and a dog or two in different
parts of the valleys . . . with a stream of water reaching the eye at all parts
on the side of the hills . . .'

Banville had hoped for three dozen birds, but the Scottish keepers
were all too busy with the grouse-shooting to give him much help,
so he came away with only nine birds one of which died on the
journey home.

'Saturday 20 of August, Leith
I got aboard all safe at 7 o'clock, the wind all fair. I had a hard task to keep
the gentlemen and ladies from looking at my feathered family. At last there
did a gentleman come up to me with four ladies and he said to me "Show
those black game to these ladies in a minute". I made no answer finding he
was a stiff man and he was making way to take off the covering, but I sent
him and his ladies [away] the same as they came and told him my game was
not fetched aboard for a show and that I had paid my fare and that I should

This keeper's gibbet would cause considerable consternation today. The species appear to include crow, possibly cuckoo, jay, sparrowhawk, one or two cats, heron, badger, possibly pine marten, and a magpie. Although he set traps for vermin, there is no record of Larry Banville being nearly so indiscriminate. There seems to be something like a live barn owl perusing the situation in the branches on the right.

not as much as allow anyone to look at them any more. Now if this man had come in a kind and civil way, he and his friends should have seen them with pleasure, but if the truth was known he thought as I was an Irishman any treatment was good enough for me.

The evening became quite dark, with a thick fog and the Captain . . . went too close to the shore and was grounded. All on board was in a fright, [but] I took my time and lay alongside of my birds. Then did a gentleman come to me and said "The vessel is ashore." I told him it was no odds to me, I was not sick which is a rare thing to me on board.'

> Banville returned to Cromer with eight black grouse, a recipe for
> Scotch broth and an exotic remedy for rheumatism which included
> substantial quantities of sweet oil, hog's lard, rum, wine and best
> brandy. Unfortunately there is a gap of ten days in the diary at this
> point and we hear no more of the black grouse. The attempt to
> breed them in Norfolk at this time was unsuccessful. Another
> attempt was made in the summer of 1837, but though the birds
> lived for several years they gradually became extinct.

> Mr Buxton returned from London in time for the opening of the
> shooting season and Larry had his first real chance of getting to
> know his new master. Apart from Sundays, there were very few
> days when there was no shooting. They shot over Sheringham,
> Cromer, Runton, Beckham and Bodham and sometimes they
> hunted for snipe on Beeston 'Bog'. There were also occasional
> shooting parties at Earlham or on Lord Suffield's estate at Gunton.
> Wherever they went Larry kept a careful account of all the game
> shot.
>   Banville found Mr Buxton and his brother-in-law, Samuel
> Hoare, easy masters to serve, but he rubbed along rather un-
> comfortably with his fellow-keepers, Davison and Ridout.

'September 1 of 1825

This morning I got orders to start for Sheringham Lodge where my master and Mr Mark Lloyd [Llewellyn Lloyd's brother and an occasional visitor to his Buxton cousins] took their breakfast [and] was waited on by Mrs Upcher and Miss Goodman . . . No breakfast was for Poor Larry although it being a fellow-keeper's house. Mr Ridout was his name. We shot at Beckham and Bodham. We hunted General and Dash for the first part of the day – the

A SOUTH EAST VIEW OF CROMER.

Another fine view of Cromer from the beach to the east, engraved from a painting by John Varley. This was the scene of many sea regattas as well as exercises for the local life-boats and experiments in sea-rescue.

birds was as wild as hawks. Not a breath of wind . . . they both shot pretty fair, 52 partridges, 2 hares, 2 rabbits – 56 head fell to the guns this day . . .

Tuesday 20 of September

This morning I was up at 5½ o'clock and went to Mr Hoare's coachman and he asked me why I was not up at 5 o'clock and walk on a few miles on the road to spare a pair of gentleman's horses that ought to be fed as well as any gentleman's in all the world . . . The butler of the name of Mr Brown told me he would do the same if he was my master. What a good thing for Poor Larry that those poor beggars was not master . . . but thanks be to God He is my provider and I have to [thank] T. F. Buxton Esq. M.P. and Samuel Hoare Esq. for their kindness to me. I was all day yesterday on foot as the reader may see, while these puffed up fellows very likely was gorging themselves with Mr John Gurney's good ale and sitting in the Hall taking their ease, while I and my master was in the turnip field wet with fatigue and the heat of the day. This coachman have not anything to carry, only skin and bone. As for the butler he have been an old soldier and, of course, he is aware of hard travelling, but it is an old saying and a true one "Put a beggar on a fine horse and he will ride as fast as the creature can go."

Thursday 29 of September

This morning I got all things ready to go out shooting. It was a fine morning. My master and I went in to Cromer. At Mr Hoare's I got orders to go to Hungry Hills. I left the shot for his Honour to carry – it was on the pony's neck – but he did not say anything to Poor Larry for so doing. I remember one time at Dunbeath Hills on Lord Dunbar's estate I done the same thing for Mr Lloyd and he swore at me enough to make me curse the day I was born from a woman.

Tuesday 8 of November

This morning I went to Sheringham where we shot in the Bodham plantations where we saw a fair share of game. We also saw a deal of woodcocks. We had 3 parsons with us for the day. It turned to wet at 2 o'clock which wet us all to the skin. I had to go home at night, never felt cold so much – at my arrival home no fire to dry my clothes or to warm myself . . . I thought my fellow keeper might [have] had a fire in the room as he had nothing else to do. The game that was bagged is 6 partridges, 7 pheasants, 7 woodcocks, 5 hares, 2 rabbits – 27 head. A cold night at 11 o'clock, cutting wadding.'

> Complaints about fellow-keepers were to feature strongly in every volume of the diary. Mr Buxton, on the other hand, knew well how to win Larry's heart, as he showed on a memorable outing to Lord Suffield's at Gunton.

'Tuesday 29 of November

This morning I got orders to get ready to go to Lord Suffield's, which I was well pleased to hear the order given to me to see the pheasants and hares as they all talk a deal about them. I rode off with my master. There were 11 guns. My master killed the game that follows, 19 pheasants, 3 woodcocks, 12 hares, 24 rabbits – 58 was his part. The [next] highest gentleman was 40 head, so he was the best in the field.

I can not help thanking my honoured master for what he done this day at lunch time. He saw that there were no lunch for me, and he put his generous paw into his lordship's bag and gave me some beef and bread and said to me "Go to that man and he will give you a glass of ale", which I did.

Partridge-shooting in the 1820s.

This day I saw James Parsons for the first time. I heard a deal about him
. . . He thinks a deal about himself. He walks after his master whose name
is Mr Grige, a very rich man. The keepers all behaved very civil to me. This
day I saw a flight of pheasants near 100 on wing together, which was a fine
sight to see.'

It had been a true November, wet and foggy, with the occasional
north-easterly wind whipping the sea into a menacing onslaught
on the Cromer cliffs. Larry had spent long hours out with his
masters or tramping alone through the dripping woods, grimly
determined to reduce the rabbit population on his territory. After
dark his time was also spent in solitary fashion, cleaning the guns
and cutting up wadding. But Larry was not to be so much alone
for long.

On 12 December 1825, Larry Banville was married to Sarah Lown.
They set up home in a Cromer cottage with a garden and enough
space to keep a pig and some poultry. Disappointingly Banville

has little or nothing to say about this house which was his first real home since he had left Ireland.

'Monday 5 of December

This was almost wet day. My love and her mother came to see the house where we were to go in when married if all do be well.

Sunday 11 of December

This day was fine. I went to Sheringham, for my name was to be asked in church for the last time. I went to Lower Sheringham where there were a ship run ashore. I was there with my intended wife, returned home with her, a fine night.

Monday 12 of December 1825

This day I was married by the Rev. Mr Pulleyne [Rector of Upper Sheringham and Headmaster of Gresham's School], paid him 7s. 6d for it, gave the ringers 12s. 6d, the clerk 5s. In all it cost me was £1. 5s. od. I was home to my house at half past 11 o'clock in Cromer which they fired off guns on that account – the day was fine and night also.

Tuesday 13 of December

This was also a fine day. I went to ferret and killed 8 rabbits, all that I saw – a fine night at nine o'clock.'

A fishing boat saving the crew of a ship in distress off Sheringham.

Sarah must soon have learnt what kind of man she had married, one who could not resist killing a few rabbits even on the day following his wedding! Larry was not an ideal husband. His drinking habits caused some quarrels between the pair and his long working hours must have been a trial to Sarah, especially after she became pregnant in the spring of 1826.

Banville guarded his coverts seven days a week, but despite the demands of his job, and despite his Catholicism, he usually found time to attend Cromer parish church on a Sunday. There he observed, with a sardonic eye, the vagaries of the clergy and the ebb and flow of the congregation according to the presence or absence of the gentry.

'Sunday 5 of February 1826

This day I went to church and it was almost empty as my master was gone . . .

Sunday 19 of February

This day it was a cold stormy morning. I went to church and heard a parson preach the same as if he was paid by the line, for I believe there were not one in the church could read as fast as he did, for scarce had the clerk time to say amen. The whole of the people appeared very cold.'

Church-going was occasionally abandoned for other pleasures.

'Sunday 26 of February

This morning I was dressed to go to church and Ridout and Woodhouse, Wyndham's keeper, came to my house and they asked me to take a pot of porter and we drank a few pots. I was drunk and sick the whole evening.'

Sunday was also the day for family walks and tea with the in-laws.

'Sunday 9 of April

. . . Miss Newson and my wife and I went up to the Lighthouse, paid 1s. to see it. It was well worth seeing.

Sunday 25 of June

Edmund Lown and his girl came to see my wife and myself. I went home and had some tea and then went down to the jetty for a walk and then we went a part of the way to the Lighthouse and we went too on the sand and then we went on the cliff, 200 foot high and my wife was in the family way 4 or 5 months which was a dreadful thing for her to do. We again returned home by the top of the cliff . . . I went up to the Hall and found out that I lost one of my ducks, and that was what I got by my visitors.'

Sarah, at mid-term in her pregnancy, was often unwell and her temper was as uncertain as the weather.

'Tuesday 11 of July

My wife and 2 of the servants went to Sheringham to Mrs Ridout's. She was not well by no means . . . I am sorry to say the pony-cart broke down there. They were forced to stop until the boy came to the Hall for the dog-cart and took them on. That was the cause of my dear wife not to be well, but thank God they are safe home at 7 o'clock.

Saturday 15 of July

My wife was bad for near 3 hours and I thought that she was went away which it was a bad thing for us both. I was forced to go out for some cold spring wash water for her. It is all right at present which I am very thankful for it . . .

Thursday 20 of July

This morning I went to Sheringham with Mr Woodgate and Mrs Kelly . . . At my arrival home my wife would not speak a word to me. She went to bed in the same mind as I found her . . .

Sunday 23 of July

This morning it was a wet day. The wind was from the eastward and a stiff gale. It made the tide as high as it have been for this 6 or 7 years past. I went to church where I heard a good sermon. After dinner I lay down and I am sorry to say that when I was asleep my wife came and tied my both feet together which I did not like at all. I am afraid that a great many partridges is drowned with the storm, for I hardly ever witnessed such weather in all my life. My wife and I went down to see the sea . . . This night looks like winter more than summer.'

Three months later Larry makes this restrained but happy entry in his diary –

'Saturday 18 of November

Last night my mother-in-law came to see my wife which she is not well. I was out at Burnt Hills the whole of the night. I came home at 6 o'clock. I

'Beeston church seen from the west', painted by the Rev. James Bulwer. Beeston Bog nearby was noted for snipe and for wild flowers. The church towers of West Runton and Cromer and the ruins of Cromer lighthouse can be seen in the background.

lay down at the Hall for a while, but was soon called and was told that my dear wife wanted me. I went, and then for the doctor. She was very ill for a good while. At half past 2 o'clock the first fruit of her womb come to this world, a son. I shall call his name Samuel as Mr Hoare wish me to do. I cannot say at this present time what I felt the whole day. I killed a small pig this day of the year 1826. The wind is to the eastward and it is cold.'

'Samuel Hoare', a watercolour of 1834 by George Richmond. Hoare was T. F. Buxton's regular shooting companion in North Norfolk.

A poacher caught red-handed.

Chapter 5

GAMEKEEPER

1826

As a keeper Banville was totally dedicated, ever anxious to kill the most rabbits, train the best dogs and preserve the most birds for his master to shoot. Poachers were his natural enemies and he records several encounters with these 'gentlemen'.

'This morning I got orders to go to Runton to shoot there and I was to take the black mare of the name of Betty. On my way to Runton there did a man tell me that he saw a dog on the hills a few minutes before, but I went all round it but did not get a view of him. On my way I met 2 gentlemen coming from Beeston in a cart with a servant and 2 dogs and 2 guns. My master came to us and at the same time Mr Cremer came and asked was there a party shooting in Runton field which there were not. My master sent young Hoare to watch them and my master told me to go after them and get their names. I had not rode far away when I met the coachman of the name of Norfolk coming tearing along saying that there were 2 gentlemen poaching on the moors.

I went in to Cromer and found the cart and dogs and man and saw some of the gentlemen, but they were no gents. They roar at me like blackguards and [said] "Tell your master he is no gentleman," which I went. Of course I came back to the Hall and told Norfolk. He got his horse and followed them, but they shot no more. They were friends of Mr James Sayers of Beeston and stopped there the night before and had my partridges I make no doubt . . .'

The second week in January 1826 brought heavy snow. Larry said 'the poor partridges was hardly able to fly with great lumps of snow from their heads to the tails'. While the snow was still on the ground Larry again heard the sound of unauthorized gunshot.

'Thursday 12 of January 1826
. . . I was going home at night-fall and I heard a gun go off and I run to see or hear about it and I seen 3 in the road, and 2 went down the cliff and the

other came [along] the road. I went up to the chap that came [along] the road and asked him who was them that went down, but he would not tell me and I got him fast by the breast and said I would bring him to my master and he then told me who they were. I went home to the Hall and this very man came to the Hall and dined at the Hall table. Was not that a fine thing to see in his Hall a man that was in company with boys shooting his partridges about one hour before?'

> Banville was also worried about the warreners employed to help keep down the rabbits. At best he suspected them of dereliction of duty and at worst of outright dishonesty.

'Tuesday 28 of February 1826

This morning I went to see if the rabbits got in to the dyke . . ., but to my surprise I found 4 traps in it set by the warrener. I then went to the other part of Runton to see what the warreners was at. They both was not gone out to ferret at 12 o'clock which I thought it very odd. They killed 6 rabbits the whole day which it is out of all bounds for 2 men to do so. I will go for 3 or 4 hours and kill from 10 to 12 rabbits . . . but they will not strive to do more for their masters than what they done . . .

Tuesday 9 of May 1826

Here is a story that I was told this day of Mr Charley Chatfield . . . All the time that he killed rabbits for me no good rabbits came to my hands, which I often asked him was there no good rabbits in Runton. This man tells me that all the good ones that he used to kill was always used to be changed for light rabbits with a son-in-law of the name of Richard Abbs which I believe to be the truth of it, but if a man will do such a trick as that he is worse than a man that would stand on the highway to rob the first that would pass by.'

> This was the laying season upon which depended the success or failure of the autumn shooting. There were slack days when Banville and Ridout shot rooks and pigeons and enjoyed the odd pot of beer, but Larry still made anxious daily visits to his favourite 'feeding places'.

'Tuesday 7 of March 1826

This morning I went to Burnt Hills and found the feed as I threw it on Monday morning. I went through all the coverts, but not a pheasant made his appearance to me. I wished myself a thousand miles from it, in fact I was the same as a man that lost his wits. I was thinking what end would become of me to have all my pheasants gone out of the coverts . . . it turned to heavy

A typical keeper of the period, with his dogs and part of the bag. Like Larry, he carries a small terrier in his game-bag. Engraved after the painting by John Frederick Herring.

wet in the evening, wet me through. I stopped at home all the evening like one that was half dead . . .

Wednesday 8 of March

This morning I went to the hill as I wished to see if any pheasants made their approach to it, which I am happy to say there were no feed to be seen . . .'

Banville also had to guard his nesting birds against the intrusions of men with dogs, women gathering sticks and boys after birds' nests. He had the power of the magistrates behind him. They held petty sessions in Cromer on alternate Mondays and Banville brought several offenders before them at this time.

'Monday 13 of March

I got 2 women out sticking in the coverts and they were the first, but it is the case with the whole of the country to do it, but they ne'er do it while John D. was keeper at Cromer Hall . . .

Monday 27 of March

I went to Runton and I found a woman out sticking and she asked me to let her go in through Davey Hills to stick which I told her not to let me catch her out any more and that there were a notice at Mr Slater's to let all the people know that I will not allow any person out sticking . . .

Thursday 13 of April

. . . I then bent my course for Burnt Hills where I saw a fair share of game and I saw 3 or 4 boys out seeking for birds' nests. I thought to cross on them, but they were well used to that plan. I however was willing to give chase to them and I set out after them and I run down by the side of a lane and at the same time one of them turned up the lane. The other I followed and told him that I would fire at him if he would not stand. I took him with his shoes one in each hand. I got him in to Cromer and asked Mr Critoph to say he would go bail for him to not go out any more, but when I looked about he was off. I set off after him, caught him again below the cliff where there were plenty of fishermen and they were not well pleased with me. I told them if anyone would tell me his name I should let him go and if not I would give him up to the officers of the peace, so they told me and I done as I said, but it was not for fear they would fire the stones at me, for if they had attempted it I should have stood in my own defence. But they all saw I had a loaded double gun in my hand. I believe that was the reason that they did not pursue the plan.

This chase was full an English mile.

Sunday 16 of April

. . . I got 2 men to watch with me as the boys is determined to go out watching and seeking for nests. I got 2 women and a child in my own fields and the men got at the other side of the manor 11 boys all in a drove. I will have some up tomorrow to see if I cannot make them stop at home on Sundays.

Monday 17 of April

The boys that I gave chase to was out of town, so I took the two women up and got 2 summons for the 2 boys . . . These 2 women that I took up the gentlemen gave a good talking to and told them that if the law was put against them they would be run to a deal of cost . . .'

It is likely that some people in Cromer regarded Banville's energetic pursuit of trespassers as a positive persecution, and his unpopularity reached a point where he risked more than hard words and foul looks. Gamekeepers were always unpopular, but a keeper who was also Irish had the scales weighted very heavily against him. Local hostility was understandable bearing in mind that the ferocious Game Laws were still in force at this time, and that a man caught netting rabbits illegally could be transported for seven years if a jury could be brought to convict him.

'Friday 21 of April

This was also a fine morning. I went to ferret and killed some rabbits then, going home to get my dinner as I wanted, I was met by Blogg that was a workman in the farm. He hit me in the nose when I was walking down the road talking to Bowman. He came behind me and I not thinking of it. It was rather hard on me.

Saturday 22 of April

. . . Saw Mr Frank Pank [Cromer farmer and surveyor] who told me he was sorry for what happened yesterday and told me that he would not give him [Blogg] any more work unless I put my name to a few lines he wrote which was for me to [say] I wished he should get his work as usual. I put my name to it of course . . .

A set of boys of Cromer abused me and I told them that I would surely make some of them pay for making game . . .

Sunday 21 of May

I asked a boy what he was doing in Mr Alsop's field and he told me that he was not there and that he would go any place for all Irishmen. I said "I will

[71]

speak to your father" and the answer that he made to me was "My father would be a damn fool to do anything to me [for an] Irishman".

This boy was about 12 or 13 years old.'

Larry made a particular enemy of a Runton man called Riseborough.

'Monday 8 of May 1826

. . . I went to the magistrates and told them Mr Riseborough was not to his word, for his dog was out as usual, which they granted a warrant for him . . .

Sunday 14 of May

I called at Mrs Slater's at Runton, got a pot of beer. Mr Riseborough came in and asked what did I do there, such a rogue as I was, and I said there is 2 rogues met, so that dropped it.

Monday 15 of May

. . . Went in to Cromer. The Reverend Parson Johnson and Mr Gunton was there, so they settled Mr Riseborough's account and when he came out he told me that there did many a keeper lose his place by selling game, so I told him I was 5 or 600 miles from home and he was at his own door and if he would bring any respectable man . . . [who] would say he was well respected in the parish he lived in I should pay for him. At night when he was passing by my house he began his abuse, so I went out and told him that if [he wanted] the law of the country I would give it to him.'

It seems that Banville, presumably while he was in Sweden, had mastered the craft of tying flies for salmon and trout fishing, and he spent much of his spare time that spring making a large supply to send to Llewellyn Lloyd in Sweden.

'Saturday 1 of April

My wife had got the fishing tackle that I often wished for this time back, 15 dozen of the best hooks and 8 hanks of the best gut, 4 trout and 4 salmon, and silver tinsel and gold also fit for the both above mentioned. This is to tie flies for L. Lloyd Esq. who is in Sweden at present.

Saturday 15 of April

. . . I finished my flies and bottom lines which they are as follows, first salmon flies 54, large trout flies 57, small trout flies 48, the whole is 159 flies, also made 12 fit lines, 6 of them single gut, 3 double and 3 treble gut and 32 bait hooks all tied on double twisted gut of the best sort, all which I mean to send to Sweden.

Sunday 16 of April
This morning I packed up all the flies with a fishing rod, sent them by Beasy's [the Cromer carriers] to go to Norwich to start off on Tuesday to Sweden.

Thursday 27 of April
This day I paid John Beasy 3 shillings for a parcel that he sent to Norwich to go to Mr Lloyd in Sweden . . .

Saturday 7 of May
. . . John Beasy was the man that my parcel was entrusted to, but he got my money and did not deliver them as he ought.'

> The precious parcel had indeed gone astray, and Banville pursued the Beasy brothers right through till the autumn, eventually applying to the magistrates to get some compensation.

'Thursday 7 of September 1826
I am sorry to say that this day brings me news that I did not like, that is that Mr Lloyd ne'er got the flies that I sent to him the 16 of April 1826. The whole was worth £9. 10s. 0., but all, all is gone I fear . . .

Monday 2 of October
. . . I went to the magistrates and saw Lord Suffield there, but he told me he could not make me get anything from Beasy only that he would give him a good talking to, but that is but little use to me . . .

Monday 9 of October
I then went to the magistrates where Beasy and his brother was. I believe they both were drunk. He said that he gave the parcel to his brother and the brother to a man at the office, but that will be proved in another week. They are all to come next Monday.

Monday 16 of October
I went off to Cromer to meet Mr Beasy and his brother, but he [the brother] did not come, but he himself [Mr Beasy] came, so we took out a summons for the brother and for J. Twates, a book-keeper in Norwich . . . I met my masters in Mr Woodrow's field and they asked me what was done now. I said the same as before, but Mr Hoare said if he took my money for the booking of the parcel he is liable to 7 years transportation. Next Monday will tell it all.

[73]

Monday 23 of October
This morning I went to Cromer and my master soon followed. Then Beasy and his father and brother came and fetched two of the biggest blackguards that he could get in Norwich to clear him. All they could say was that one of them saw Beasy taking it in to the yard and coming out without it, so that was a lame story. My master asked him to pay for it, but he would not . . .'

> Larry carried this nagging grievance with him during the summer and autumn of 1826, but his mind was seldom away from the progress of his game birds. The first young birds had been sighted by Mr Clowes, the Rector, as early as 6 May, but most of the eggs did not hatch until June. Larry watched anxiously over the hatching and apparently paid small sums for eggs from deserted nests.

'Friday 2 of June
I went the way of Runton. I saw 1 pheasant's nest hatched out with 4 young ones, another all taken away by the rooks. I went to Mr Woodrow's and found that Riseborough's pig was after eating all the partridges' eggs that was in his garden . . .

Sunday 4 of June
Mr Goves told me that he got a partridge's egg that a man and woman dropped out of their pockets in the road. I must know that he is a liar and the truth is not in him . . .

Wednesday 7 of June
. . . This day I saw the first young pheasants. I wish them good success . . .

Monday 19 of June
. . . This morning I was called at 2 o'clock by a man that had 22 partridges' eggs in his hat. He cut them out of the hay as he was mowing the field.

Wednesday 28 of June
This evening I was speaking to a woman that found 2 partridges' nests on the dykes, but I told her that I could not pay for nests on the dykes. She swore at me and said if she had known that she would have eat them all, and I don't know but she [did] eat them.'

> June had been very hot and dry, but the weather broke up violently at the end of the month.

'Tuesday 27 of June
This was a fine day as yesterday was. The ground is so hot that it is enough to make any man's feet blister when walking about. The corn is all going into

the earth again. There was thunder and lightning this evening and it was enough to frighten anyone . . . It appears like wet now. I saw 4 acres of hay all put on one wagon which was a poor thing for the farmer.

Thursday 29 of June
. . . I went with my wife to Aylmerton, then crossed the fields to Runton, found the lanes and places all covered with the gravel that was taken by the fall of water yesterday. One field of barley was levelled to the earth with the flood, also the water run into one house and there were above 2 feet of water in it . . .'

On the last day of the month news arrived that Thomas Fowell Buxton had been re-elected to Parliament. His Tory opponents retained their majority under Lord Liverpool, but he headed the poll at Weymouth despite the attempts by a Tory mob to prevent the Whigs from voting. Cromer celebrated in fine style when the news of his re-election arrived.

'Friday 30 of June
This morning I did receive the glad tidings that my honoured master again was returned as a Member which it was a day of great mirth in this part. The guns was fired, the colours flying in all parts of the town. Mr Clowes spoke for us all and told that the reason that my master was put in again was that the freeholders wish him well. They all drank to Mr Buxton's good health and no slavery, which I wish it may be the case with all my heart. I then went to my coverts to look round. I did not go to drink any of the money that was gave to make them a frolic. The money was £2 that was given by the gentlemen.

The colours was turned upside down to tell the people that they were all in distress. It was done in a joke – they were all getting hearty. But I called at the Hall, took my wife home after I had the honour to drink to my master's health with a glass of wine.'

There was another excuse for celebration in Cromer ten days later when young George Wyndham came of age. Since his father's death eleven years earlier, he had been the owner of Cromer Hall and of the estates of the Cromer branch of the Wyndham family. At the age of nineteen he had fallen in love with Maria Windham, one of the younger daughters of Admiral Windham who inherited the

The 17th-century Felbrigg Hall, seat of Admiral Windham in Banville's day.
This picture was engraved by J. Walker in 1798 from a drawing by the great landscape
gardener, Humphry Repton.

nearby Felbrigg estate in 1824. Family objections had held up the marriage, but on obtaining his majority, he wasted no time in marrying her. Their wedding took place in the second week of July 1826.

'Monday 10 of July
This was a day of great mirth in Cromer with poor and rich. Mr George Wyndham came of age and came into Cromer the same as if he was the king of it. Mr Sandford [Captain of the life-boat] and a few more gentlemen was standing at a corner and they asked me what did I think of that. I told them it was well, but they used his honour too much before they knew him, which they laughed at me. There were 2 barrels of beer given away from each house in Cromer; 5 public houses was in it at this day. They drank it; there was good order keeped in the field. Mr Ridout was also there – he was very full which I was ashamed of.

Wednesday 26 of July
This morning I got a rabbit and rat in my traps and Charles Chatfield got a young hare which was a good thing as I wanted it for the house as the family

is at home this day. I wish I could hear from my old master and also my aged father, but there is no sign of it at present. I did not see one young partridge this day . . .'

> With the return of his master from Weymouth, Larry's spirits improved and some pleasant summer days followed.

'Saturday 5 of August
. . . I spoke to my master and he told me there were plenty of partridges in the county . . . he also told me that he was to send my favourite dog to Mr Lloyd in Sweden. I wish him good sport over him. He also told me to feed in all my feeding places which that I liked above all things.

Sunday 20 of August
This day I walked a good deal and I saw the fields all covered with ladybirds, a kind of silly fly. They are in millions on the east . . .

Thursday 24 of August
I started off to Beeston where we pulled out an old boat that was in the pond and . . . then we drew the ponds and got out some fish, very fine ones. My master ordered 6 of the best of them to be keeped out. We then started off to

Retrieving a cock pheasant.

the Heath Lodge where there were lunch for them, a small part for Poor Larry. It was outside of the back door that it was given to us.

From there to Mr Withers of Holt [the attorney], but on our way we drew a pond at Bodham town pits, but got no fish. We got a deal of fish out of the pond at Holt, came with them to Beeston all packed up in dry wheaten straw all done well. I take some of them home to Cromer and they were in as good order as if they were not out of the water 5 minutes. The distance is about 12 miles.'

> Though happy in his work Larry was concerned for Sarah as she drew nearer her time. He was also worried by the arrival on the scene of James Parsons of whom he had formed an impression at the Gunton shoot the previous autumn. He was a man as unlike Banville in character as can possibly be imagined. From September 1826 until the summer of 1827 the two men worked side by side as fellow-keepers on the Cromer manor. There can be no doubt that Banville saw Parsons as a rival from the very beginning. To Larry's eyes James Parsons frequently seemed conceited, lazy and smooth-tongued. On the other hand he was a big man with plenty of vitality, good company and a good shot, almost as good as Banville. In a perverse way they seemed to enjoy their rivalry. He was certainly preferable to the drunken Ridout.

'Saturday 16 of September 1826
This morning I set out with the dog-cart to Sheringham where they shot over Gin and Corrowe, a Irish setter, a beauty, also little Dash, a spaniel. My master said that he is the best one that he ever saw out in his life. I believe it is.

Wednesday 20 of September
James Parsons was out with his dogs today. He thinks they are the best in the country. I killed 1 partridge, 1 rabbit. James fired but did not kill.

Thursday 12 of October
After the shooting we all dined at Mrs U's – had a good dinner. After dinner we went down into town where we had a pot of beer and my brother-in-law, William Lown, was rather hearty and himself and Ridout was talking about something or other, but at last Mr Ridout threw a glass of beer into his face and I went between them, but Ridout took up a pint porter pot, threw it at my brother-in-law over my shoulder and hit the back of my hand and him in the cheek, cut both of us. They were going to fight, but I told them [they] should not and if they wanted to fight I would wet the best of them and make

[78]

Cupet take away my brother-in-law and put him in the stocks, but it was all soon over . . .

Tuesday 17 of October
I cleaned all the guns, got wadding and all things ready for the gentlemen and James Parsons amusing himself within. At the time he came, the gentlemen wanted the guns and he asked me if they were ready. If it was my case I would be ashamed of it.

Friday 20 of October
This was a dark morning. I was up at half past 2 o'clock. I went to the Hall, found James taking his ease in his bed. I cleaned the guns, I also cut the wadding, then went off to the feeds . . . I saw a deal of the Danish crakes coming over this day. They all keeped their left wing in the wind. I saw thousands of fieldfares this morning . . .

At night I found my wife not well by no means. Mr C. Earle [the Cromer doctor] is going to Sheringham; he is to tell my mother-in-law to come to us this night if all is well with her. There is 2 children bad with the fever next door.

Sunday 22 of October
This morning I was not well in my mind. My wife was bad all night. I sat at the fireside all night. 5 o'clock I went up to the Hall and lay down for a while . . .

Wednesday 25 of October
. . . My honoured master offered me anything that his house could afford for my wife, which is very kind of him to do so . . .'

The following Monday Banville accompanied his master on a shooting expedition to Earlham Hall. Miss Glover, the Buxtons' governess, went with them and asked Larry if he would show her his account of his travels to Sweden.

'. . . I told her not, nor would I show it to anyone yet.'

Banville claimed that he was hardly well enough to stand that day, but he 'weathered the storm out' and 'came home with flying colours'. James's industry during his absence came up to expectations.

'Wednesday 1 of November
I stopped at home to see after my feeds. 3 of them James ne'er went to the 2 days he was at home. He is a fine keeper before his master, but behind his

back he is a gentleman like all the rest of the keepers in this part of the globe . . .

Wednesday 6 of December .
My fellow-keeper cleaned one gun this evening, but did not touch the other as it was my master's. I always clean all guns when I go at them, but he cleaned it while I was at home keeping my wife company for the space of one hour. I packed the game on the hooks and it is full an hour's work and I also fed the dogs this night. He put up the game in the game larder last night as I was with my master and left out 12 snipes, 2 woodcocks. The rats ate the whole.

Friday 15 of December
My master . . . told me that there were a set of poachers at Heydon Hall. They shot his Lordship's son. There were 25 in the gang, none of them I believe were taken . . . [Twelve men were eventually brought to trial for this attack on Lord Kensington's son. In March 1827 they were condemned to death with a recommendation for mercy.]

Sunday 17 of December
This morning I got up and fed my pheasants and got all things ready, for I was going to have my first born babe christened. I was going to get my breakfast and saw Mr Ridout and his eldest daughter to stand for my child. I did not like it by no means as I asked his wife to do it, but he is very fond of his beautiful daughter Martha.'

Banville had many reasons to feel satisfied at the end of 1826. Sarah was well recovered, he had a fine baby son and he liked his new master. The year ended with a number of parties.

'Monday 25 of December
This day I went to the Hall and I went to the church. There were a deal of people there and half of them sleeping. Mr Clowes preached. I spent the evening at the Hall and there were all things there that any man could wish for.'

This fine picture of partridges in early autumn, by Archibald Thorburn, shows how much rough ground there was and explains why partridges were so numerous compared with today. There were also plenty of thistles for goldfinches.

'Pheasants in the Spring' by Archibald Thorburn.

ANGLING.

1. Phantom Minnow. SALMON FLIES. 2. Totnes Minnow.

3. Caddis.

5. March Brown.

7. Jock Scott. 8. Pennell's Pattern.
(Gold Bodied)

4. Caddis Fly.
or Stone Fly

6. May Fly.

TROUT FLIES.

Brown Palmer 10. Stone Fly. 11. Grey Drake. 12. Brown Moth. 13. Red Spinner. 14. Black Gnat 15. Willow Fly. 16. Whirling Dun.

Then on Boxing Day there was a rabbiting party, '6 men, 3 boys, 9 dogs' and 'a gallon of beer' to reward their labours. The following evening they ran races.

'This evening James Parsons ran against the coachman about 58 yards. He also ran against William Cook – he was beat the twice.'

This gratifying defeat no doubt softened Larry's heart towards his rival, for James Parsons was one of the guests at a small party the Banvilles gave on New Year's Eve.

'Mr Norfolk [the coachman] and 2 children, and husband and Mrs Kelly [the housekeeper] came to my house and Mr Woodgate and James Parsons also. We spent a merry time of it. Past 11 o'clock, a dark night.'

Larry's hand-tied flies were a labour of love, and there was grievous distress when a box of flies for the family was lost or stolen. His flies may have been less standard and orthodox than these, but they were probably just as effective.

[81]

PART II

A NORFOLK LIFE

1827–1836

Chapter Six

COMPANIONS

1827–29

During the next ten years, 1827 to 1836, Banville's diaries cover a number of different aspects of Norfolk life. They give a vivid picture of how the young Irishman fitted into the tightly knit world of the Buxtons, their neighbours, and their retainers.

Although Larry cannot have been an easy companion, his fellow-keepers always found him a good sportsman out in the field and an excellent story-teller. Everyone in the local circle enjoyed his professional skills and his company, though they might have been surprised by some of his comments on them in his diary.

When the Buxtons left Cromer Hall and moved to Northrepps, Banville moved too, and eventually set up house in Sheringham. But on the whole Larry is reticent about his own family and writes far more about the Buxtons and their fortunes during this decade. At the end of it, in 1836, he returned to his home in Ireland for a brief holiday. The chapters which follow each reflect one of these elements in Banville's life at this time.

By 1827 the young Irish keeper was a familiar figure on the Cromer landscape. Well known to many, it is difficult to say how many real friends he had. His hours of work were long and many of his tasks were solitary by nature, so he perhaps had few opportunities to build up the friendships that grow naturally out of shared pleasures. It was specially unfortunate that he was unable to feel genuine liking for any of his fellow-keepers, for with them he did have opportunities for a little sport. On pretext of keeping down the vermin they could shoot rabbits, rats, pigeons and sparrows, and enjoy a little nocturnal ferreting. Best of all were the days when they got away for a little wildfowling.

During 1827 and 1828 Banville's chief companions in these

activities were George Ridout and James Parsons. Ridout appears in the diary as a rather weak character, often the worse for drink which made him surly and sometimes violent. At least once he was involved in a public house brawl which resulted in broken chairs and tables. Larry found it difficult to respect such a man. James Parsons, as we have already seen, excited Banville's jealousy and aroused all his competitive instincts. The three men together must have made an interesting trio when they set out for Barton Broads on the morning after All Fools' Day 1827.

'Sunday 1 of April 1827

James Parsons . . . and George Ridout intend to go to Barton Broads to shoot. They both say that they will kill 25 brace of snipes. If I will kill 4 or 5 brace I will be well pleased with the sport of the day . . .

Monday 2 of April 1827

This morning we were up early and we started off for Barton Broads. We called at the first toll bar, was forced to stop there for 8 or 10 minutes and the man came at last with the intent to take the gate off the hinges, but a boy came . . . which let us through . . . Called at Mr P.'s, got some beer and bread too . . . Then we started off to North Walsham [where] we stopped to take our breakfast . . . I will talk about the sport of the day. It was mostly in leaping drains with a pole which I was well accustomed to in my own country. Mr Ridout fell in up to the middle. The ground was all covered with wet which made the snipes as wild as hawks. We killed 3 snipes each of us and 1 snipe between Parsons and myself, which it makes up 5 brace instead of 50 brace . . . I did laugh at my 2 companions as they were to do such feats, but they have not travelled as far as I did. I shot a pike this day. I shot at another, but did not kill it.'

> Banville mentions some other pastimes in his diary including cricket, bowls, three pins and cock-fighting, but the impression given is that Norfolk men took most of their pleasure in drinking and sometimes in bare-knuckle fighting. On one occasion such a fight reached the level of a public entertainment.

'Tuesday 5 of June 1827

. . . I then went to stop rabbits out of the fields at Compit Hills. I was not long at the work when a great crowd of people was passing the way of my barns . . . I sent John Bolding to ascertain what they were going about and he told me that the Admiral Windham's keepers was going to fight James Leake of Runton and Joseph Salmon of Cromer, which I went to see them.

WILD FOWL SHOOTING

These wildfowlers on the Broads seem to be going through huge reed beds (artists' licence, no doubt) and have a punt-gun mounted in the boat. At Hickling and Horsey they would have shot swans, several species of duck, and coots.

George Bird came to me, said that they would fight on my manor, but I told him if he would I should fetch a summons against him, that they had a manor of their own and to fight on it but not on mine. I also told him not to fight, if he would that he would not gain anything by it, but his answer was he would fight Leake. I also told him he would be beat, [but] all was to no use. They fought for a long time, but Leake came off the best. Peter Langdon also fought. He was beat too, so the keepers went off all beat in style which it was a good thing for them, for Peter was a big block by all accounts by all that knew him . . .'

None of the combatants was any the worse for the fight and the defeat of the keepers seems to have given satisfaction all round. James Leake was the Runton blacksmith and already had a considerable reputation for strength and endurance. The following entry appeared in the *Norwich Mercury* for 24 February 1827.

'A short time since, James Leake, a son of Vulcan, who resides at Runton, near Cromer, having one of his toes which caused

[87]

him great uneasiness from having been previously hurt, he determined on cutting it off – but fearing the expense of calling in a surgeon, he manufactured an instrument for the express purpose, and, without any assistance, performed the operation himself, and at one blow the toe was separated from the foot. The profusion of blood was immense, to prevent which he seared the stump with a hot iron. The wound is healing fast and Leake is in perfect health.'

It seemed that toughness and insensitivity of varying kinds were characteristics of the Leake family. A Miss Leake was a milliner established at Leake's Cottage, Cromer. Every year in the *Norwich Mercury*, she 'humbly solicited the attention' of the ladies of Cromer to her 'elegant display of Parisian and London millinery, dresses, corsets and flowers etc.' but Banville repeats in his diary a less savoury tale about her and her brother which was current in 1829.

'Friday 17 of April 1829
Mrs Brambury and her daughter was here this day and told me the awfullest tale that I ever heard in all my life. It is of Miss Leake of Cromer that have 4 young women dress-makers that are learning of her. They all board themselves and she keeps a little girl to do the work and she . . . got a bit of one of the girls' plum cake and eat of it . . . Miss Leake and her dear brother Thomas Leake got stuff to make this poor child throw it up. Tom held the child while this dress-maker, Miss Leake, poured it into the child's throat. The girl's name was Miss Bathsheba Pegg of Lower Sheringham, Norfolk, that lost the morsel of cake. The child was a poor man's of the name of Mathis of Northrepps.'

The picnic was a popular form of relaxation with all classes at this time, and Norfolk then, as now, offered many delightful settings for such outings. Several picnics are described in the diary and two of the best come from the summer of 1827. It was a promising season; the turnips, as Larry observed, were looking well all over the county and the wheat harvest had begun early. In cheerful mood a party of servants from the Hall set out to enjoy what Banville calls a 'gipsy party' (the word is difficult to decipher).

[88]

'Thursday 26 of July 1827

This morning we all got ready at the Hall to go to Beeston as a gipsy party, so we all rode off on donkeys. I rode with a Scotch plaid and a cap of fox-skin that master shot in Sweden, L.Lloyd Esq. I mean. We all arrived there in good order. The whole people that saw us as we passed through Runton and Beeston cheered us the same as if we were a noble people as we were going, but they all was laughing at us on our return as the evening turned to such a wet one. Indeed I was wet through and so was the whole party. It is often the case that people go to mock others and get mocked theirselves . . . I believe each of us paid from 5s. 6d. to 7s. 6d. which was a great plenty to pay for a day's pleasure. Edward Bowman strained his ankle which made the day not pleasant for us all . . . we were all quite tired of the journey. My wife was so as she had a child. Miss Newson took the greatest care of her . . . The whole of the afternoon was . . . as cold as I could wish for. This day I lost my pipe which I am sorry for it.'

One feels that Larry was not altogether at ease with such junketings!

The second great picnic that summer was a Buxton affair, a grand family outing with Larry acting as chef of the day. It was a jolly occasion, though again the pleasure was not completely unalloyed.

'Friday 3 of August 1827

This was a fine day. We all started off to Barton Broads to fish and sport for the day. There were in the first place 22 in the party. I was the cook of the fish. My master often called to me to put plenty of salt and pepper on the fish as I was roasting it on the fire of turf near the fishing place. The postman of the name of Cockright got drunk, but he came the whole way pretty well until we came to Northrepps toll bar. My master ordered me to get off and take off his leaders as he was riding. I was sorry for it. I told my master that he was not a man that had his right senses this evening. [This] thing spoiled the whole. My wife was not well pleased with me this night. It is out of a man's power to please a woman when she thinks fit to be in a bad mind. It is a bad thing for anyone to get tipsy when they have a gentleman and ladies to dine, but the day was very fine and very hot the whole of it which made him get drunk.'

Pike-fishing in the 1820s.

Dour and detached Larry may have appeared on some of these social occasions, but he undoubtedly had his strong points as a companion on long hunting and shooting expeditions. His skill as a raconteur must have become well known to Ridout and Parsons, just as it later came to be treasured by Buxton in long hours waiting in the heather for Highland deer. Larry had a fund of curious anecdotes, collected from many sources, which he wrote into his diary from time to time. Some were spine-chilling tales of the supernatural, others were horror stories of cruelty to children or animals, but many simply illustrated the extraordinary quirks of human behaviour from which Banville was often pleased to draw an improving moral. One concerned Lord Townshend.

'Here is a story that a servant told us this evening. He lives with Lord Townshend of Rainham Hall . . . His lordship used to send this man 10 miles for a lemon that used to cost 6d, but he took the opportunity of bringing home 4 and gave in one of them. The next day the order came out for him to start for another lemon, [so] he gave in [another] one, and his lordship asked if he went for it to town, which his answer was "I brought 3 spare ones yesterday". Then his lordship returned in and wrote a note to send to

Swaffham which [is] 12 miles further than Fakenham. At his arrival there, to his great astonishment, he found it was for a pennyworth of tape, [so] he put up the horse and got some refreshment, stopped a while in the town and when he returned home his lordship gave orders that he should speak to him. He went to bed, but he was obliged to get up again and go to his lordship. "What kept you out so long?" [he asked]. "Because I was obliged to wait as the man could not get such a large order ready for your lordship in a moment!" I think this is one of the oddest stories that ever was heard of in any country.'

Larry could also tell of the perils of cigar-smoking.

'I was told the other day that Mr Hurry who is lodging in Cromer was smoking a cigar and Mrs Upcher of Sheringham was driving right after him. He thought it not right to smoke the ladies as one of her daughters was with her. He put it out, as he thought, and happened to put it into his pocket and a powder-horn [was] in it. The fire and powder could not agree. Off it went and floored the gentleman and upset the ladies, but no harm took place but the loss of the horn and also the skirt of his coat. Let this be a warning for all smokers.'

Or he could suggest a cure for laryngitis.

'There were a young woman in Cromer that got cold and all the doctors could do nothing for her and she lost her speech, but Mrs. Langham cured her by the following medicine. She took a pint of strong beer and put it by the fire and roasted a herring and let fat drop into it. She drank it as hot as she could which by that means she got her speech again which was a good thing.'

Larry brought home some blood-curdling stories from his Swedish friends.

'Alas, it happened that a ship, a Danish ship, came ashore by foul wind and was obliged to shore there and these three men and a boy was in the habit of going to them with milk and eggs . . . to sell. The Captain always dealt with them and was very good to them. It happened one morning, they rode alongside of the vessel and asked for a drink of water that they were very dry. But he, being of a good mind, ordered them up on deck and fetched them up a bottle and said to them, "Drink plenty". When he was in the act of giving a glass to one of them, he was knocked down and all of the crew shot, which was three men and a poor little boy – he ran up the rigging but he they served the same.

Then they robbed the vessel of all that they could take with them. They sold a great part to the people in the neighbourhood. Then did word go to Gothenburg that there were a vessel on shore and that the crew was all killed. The men that went to watch the ship saw fishermen on the spot and the things that was sold them was the same as the vessel was laden with which made them all look for their boat. They got it up and the blood was all on it. One of those men came up and gave himself up and said, "I am willing to die for the crime" and told them who was with him at the time. He longed for the hour of death, but it was not the case with the other two for they would not confess for near six months after him. He sang psalms up to the place and then stripped himself and then wished them all "Good-bye" and kissed the clergyman that came with him and shook hands with two more and he then lay down. The man came to chop off his hand and head and the axe stuck so in the block so that one of the clergy was forced to lay his foot on it and the poor fellow ne'er stirred a bit. He was not as much as noticed to shrink a bit at his hand being taken off. At the time that this man's head was cut off, to the surprise of all that was standing by, a man sprang into the ring and a cup in his hand and held the head over it and got some of the blood and drank, for this reason – he had the falling sickness and he was told if he would drink some of a man's blood that was beheaded for murder, it would not come to him any more.'

But the most curious tale of all was told to him by Mr Buxton himself.

'Then he, in his droll way, told me of a gentleman in Devonshire [who] had a favourite old horse and his name was Jack. The children used to feed him with bits of bread. They brewed the beer and happened to lay the grains and beer so that Jack got at it and in the morning found the old fellow dead. They skinned him and in the evening as usual he woke from his drunken sleep and as usual came to the children for the bread. He got the butcher [to] kill half a dozen sheep, sewed the skins on Jack and he lived for many a year . . . T. F. Buxton said it was a clergyman told him the story.'

Banville's daily contacts with Parsons and Ridout were soon to be reduced. In 1827 Buxton acquired the shooting rights at Weybourne and James Parsons was sent to take charge of the new manor. This eased the day-to-day tension between him and Larry, but it did nothing to lessen their keen rivalry in the field of sport. Banville's other fellow-keeper, George Ridout, was soon to disappear from the pages of the diary altogether. His resort to the bottle seems to have become more frequent during 1828, and at last his drinking overstepped the bounds of his master's tolerance and he was given notice. His dismissal brought on a further bout of drinking.

'Friday 26 of December 1828

This morning my master gave me orders to go to Sheringham and Weybourne [and] find up Ridout and Parsons to shoot . . . On my way I met Ridout at Mrs Pegg's [beerhouse]. From [there to] Weybourne, found James near 2 miles from the house. I walked on and he rode back for his gun . . . All went on very well until my master asked Ridout did he give the game out? He said he did give 3 pheasants . . . My master said he told him they were for James P., and Ridout said that his honour did not tell him and they had a few hot words. My master told him to go home and he, Ridout, said he was deserving everything to strive to please him, but it was all in vain for him, so he was ordered to give up his gun, but he begged my master's pardon and wished to go with him. The whole of it was Ridout was a little the worse for porter that he drank. The day passed off very well after that . . . I did not fire a shot at the woodcocks for it put me out this day more than I have been ever since I came to the country to hear Ridout give such answers to so worthy a master as T. F. Buxton Esq. is, I was ashamed of it.'

> We hear little more of poor Ridout, but James Parsons remains a major character in the diary for many years to come. Larry sometimes visited him for a little sport on the Weybourne muds. We hear of James Parsons boasting in the Weybourne pub that he will outshoot Larry and of Larry's satisfaction when he fails to do so. We hear of James courting the daughter of John Lance, a butler, but with no serious intention of matrimony.

'Thursday 22 of January 1829

In the evening we went from Stiffkey sluices to the town. The butler came and had a glass of grog with us, then we took a walk up the streams. We got one duck which the butler took home with him, but I think I killed it. The butler claimed it . . . James Parsons was courting his daughter, but I believe he will not have her for a wife.

Friday 23 of January

There were plenty of game at Stiffkey sluices. If I had not wet my foot I would have killed a deal of ducks.'

The character of Parsons seems instantly recognizable. How like
Parsons, one feels, is this little incident from January 1829.

'This morning James Parsons came to the Hall and went to get a long gun
from Lord Suffield's. He got the gun; we then started off to Weybourne in
James's gig, and at Beeston there were a drift of snow and I said to James,
"Let us get out." But he drove at it the more, fell and broke the 2 shafts off
at the body of the gig. Let this be a warning for all that will it see to not drive
at a drift of snow with 2 men in a gig.'

Chapter Seven

THE GENTRY

1825–36

Social barriers between servants and masters in late Georgian England were clear-cut and not to be overstepped. Banville never doubted that he was a servant, and though his mind was free to criticize his master's behaviour, he was careful not to deviate from the proper deportment of a servant. Nevertheless, as a keeper, he shared daily in the favourite sport of his masters and was in a position to observe their character very closely. For many years the close family life of the Buxtons and Hoares was the regular background to Larry's life, and during the years between 1829 and 1835 he saw almost as much of the Upchers. He came into contact with many of their visitors, Lloyds, Gurneys and miscellaneous clergy and MPs invited down to Norfolk for the shooting. He was also able to get significant glimpses of the neighbouring families, and his diary entries during the first ten years in Norfolk reflect the prejudices of his class for or against the masters who ruled their lives.

Despite his occasional grumbles Larry clearly loved and respected the Buxtons. He saw most of Mr Buxton, 'the best of masters', and the boys, Edward North and Harry in the early years, and Charles and Thomas Fowell II when they grew old enough to shoot with him. But he also had good things to say of Mrs Buxton's generosity to the poor, and of the goodness of Miss Priscilla.

Almost as one family with the Buxtons were the Hoares, Sam and Louisa and their eight children, six boys and two girls. Banville regarded Samuel Hoare almost equally as his master. Sam Hoare was a Lombard Street banker. Both he and Louisa were Quakers when they married, but were later received into the Church of England. Sam Hoare gave every possible support to the good causes espoused by the Buxtons, and was himself a regular visitor to the Refuge for the Destitute in Hoxton. Louisa, one of the most humorous and lively of the Gurney girls, was keenly interested in education and wrote essays on the subject.

Both families were deeply involved in evangelical and philanthropic movements of many kinds: Bible and Missionary Societies, the Association for Shipwrecked Sailors, the establishment of schools, prison reform, the emancipation of the slaves and the promotion of Christian values in all walks of life. They were naturally Whigs in politics, though much more truly liberal than many Whigs of the day.

There were other members of the family nearby who shared fully in all the family enthusiasms. Northrepps Cottage was the charming home of the learned and charitable spinsters, Sarah Maria Buxton and Anna Gurney. Sarah was Thomas Fowell's sister and Anna was a cousin of Hannah and Louisa. They were known as 'the Cottage Ladies', universally loved and respected for their public work, and there will be more to say of them in a later chapter.

Many other kindred spirits from the locality were drawn into the Buxton family circle. Charlotte Upcher, the widow, and her young family at Sheringham Hall, the Reverend Clowes and his sister at Colne House, Cromer, and several local gentlemen clergy of the evangelical persuasion were both friends and fellow workers in good causes. Larry knew them all and passed his own private judgements on them.

Banville was also in a position to observe and record his reactions to some of the older county families. On shooting expeditions to neighbouring estates he saw much of Lord Suffield at Gunton, and of the Windhams of Felbrigg and their relations the Wyndhams of Cromer. Lord Suffield was in every way a natural friend and ally of the Buxtons and Hoares. He shared their political views and gave timely support to many of their causes in the House of Lords. He campaigned vigorously for the reform of the vicious Game Laws and had already secured the outlawing of spring-guns. There can be no doubt that from the point of view of the Buxtons, Hoares and Banville himself, Lord Suffield was on the side of the angels.

Wildfowling on the Norfolk coast. Larry used to go with his fellow-keepers to shoot duck on the saltings between Wells and Weybourne, usually at the mouth of the Stiffkey river.

Punt-gunning on ice on the Broads was a back-breaking operation, but it was quite effective to put skids on a punt and drag or push oneself over the ice after duck. Few people, if any, do it today.

The same cannot be said of the Windhams of Felbrigg. The owner of Felbrigg Hall in Banville's time was Vice-Admiral William Windham. He was born William Lukin and was the eldest son of the half-brother of William Windham III, the great Parliamentarian and member of Pitt's war Cabinet. When Windham died childless in 1810 he named William Lukin as his heir, but left the house and estate at Felbrigg to his widow, Cecilia, during her lifetime. At her death in 1824 William Lukin changed his name to Windham and moved from his family home at Felbrigg Parsonage into the Hall, a beautiful 17th-century mansion filled with a treasury of fine pictures and furniture.

The new owner of Felbrigg had had a fairly distinguished naval career, though his elevation to the rank of Vice-Admiral had been in the nature of a retirement gift. In politics he was a Whig of the old school. In answer to a friend who claimed he was 'a reformer and no Whig', Windham proudly answered that he was 'a Whig and no reformer'. He was on the opposite wing of the party to the Buxtons and Hoares, and socially he regarded them to some extent as interlopers in Norfolk society.

In a characteristic letter to his nephew, the Reverend Cremer, he wrote

'. . . I really, my dear Cremer, want no man's land; but what I want, though I should not like *publicly* to hold that language, is to keep such men as Hoare away if possible, and there is no reasonable sacrifice that I would not make to effect that object. This you may say savours of feudality, but if it does, it has a due regard to old proprietors and to the names. I like and always have liked what may be termed, I hope without arrogance, native consequency, and I am always tenacious of its invasion, and hence my dislike of Cromer. There is certainly in the human mind a natural desire to level everybody above us to our own standard, coupled as it always is with a proportionate desire of not lowering ourselves or of elevating others up to us; and it is from this natural propensity of our minds that I dislike such men as Hoare and others, under the mask of a watering-place come among us . . .'

Although polite relations were maintained in public, it is possible that Banville and the other servants sensed and resented this

Snipe-shooting in the early 19th century at Barton.

attitude of the Windhams to their masters. Certainly Vice-Admiral Windham, whom the Norfolk historian and last private owner of Felbrigg, R. W. Ketton-Cremer, described as 'a genial and kindly man', was heartily disliked by Banville for a number of reasons.

The Admiral had a large family of children including six daughters for whom he had to find husbands. His choice of a husband for Cecilia did not meet with local approval.

'Saturday 10 of July 1825

This day was rather wet. I did not do much. A deal of people went to Felbrigg Hall to see a great dinner that was to be given away this day, but who was it to be given away to? Why, gentle folks of course.

I returned home with my 3 rabbits and found all those people that went to see these great doings at Felbrigg Hall very much disappointed . . . It was a great wedding between Mr Baring [a widower, banker and ex-MP] and Miss Windham of Felbrigg Hall. Her age was 21 or 22 years and his age was 65 or 66 as the people do say. She was crying the most of the day. It rained a part of the day. She is going away with her old man. His daughter looks as fit for his wife as the wife he have got.'

Maria, as we have seen, was luckier and made a love match with her cousin George Wyndham, but another daughter was being hopefully displayed at Gunton in 1827.

'Friday 7 of December 1827

This morning my master and I rode to Lord Suffield's which we rode very fast, but we were there before they started off to shoot . . . The Admiral Windham, while we were all getting ready, he was walking his daughter up and down before the Hall door for the gentlemen to see her . . .

This day I helped the gentlemen over the dyke that there were a good deal of water in it and I thought . . . that I ought to let the old Admiral in to it, but it is all past away.'

A few years later a further daughter was to be sacrificed to an elderly man of means.

'Saturday 26 of July 1834

I heard those guns at Felbrigg Park firing as one of the Miss Windhams was married to Sir William Cook. He tied up to the bride £2,000 a year for her life. This was the day for the bride not for the bridegroom as Old Nick might have the old heap of bones only for the gold. She is 23 years and he is 63. What a difference.'

[98]

Shooting a cock pheasant.

No doubt an added reason for the Admiral's unpopularity was the enclosure of the parishes of Felbrigg, Aylmerton, Metton, Sustead and Gresham which took place in 1826. Banville was probably echoing popular opinion when he wrote

'. . . He, poor devil, is stealing all from them and throwing down all the houses in his parishes to send the poor out of it. If the Lord of all is just in his sayings what will become of that man that oppress the poor, because he that oppress the poor oppress the Son of Man.'

The Admiral's eldest son, Mr W. H. Windham, also met with Banville's disapproval.

'Saturday 28 of January 1826
This was as fine a day as anyone could wish for. We shot at Davey Hills where we found a fair share of game. We then started off to Burnt Hills. We also found plenty of game. Mr W. Windham shot so bad and crippled so many pheasants that I at last told his honour if he could not bag them to not shoot at them as it was spoiling all of them and he was after hitting 5 one after the other and all went off.'

Young Windham was also present at a notable exchange of words between Larry and the elderly Mr Baring.

[99]

'Wednesday 5 of September 1827

This was also a fine shooting day. I was out with Master H. Buxton, a keen sportsman although only a child . . . In the course of the day I saw a party of gentlemen sporting on a part of my manor which I left Master Buxton and I went to them and addressed them as follows, "Gentlemen I come to say that you are over the bounds of your manor." By that Mr Baring said to me "You are [an] Irish blackguard," and things that he thought of and that he would tell Mr Buxton of it and that if he was a gentleman of the County he would give me such a beating that I ne'er got in my life and that I was fit for nothing only to be put aboard of a King's ship where I would be flogged well. I told this gentleman that no-one had any right to beat me. One of the young Windhams said if I would be saucy to Mr Baring he would kick my arse, so I looked hard at him and said "You kick my arse? What a fine thing for gentlemen to come to shoot a man's game and then their keeper to take it away and then tell him that they [will] kick [him]." But they all knew better, but Mr Baring said if he had his keeper with him that was in Dorsetshire he would make him kick me all round the field. Which my answer was that he would find [it] a rum job to do it as the field was so large. I believe there were near 100 acres without a few, but all is over. My master was afraid that I said anything to offend the gentleman. He is to shoot with my master tomorrow if all do be well, so then my doom will be at a end.

10 o'clock, troubled mind.

Thursday 6 of September 1827

This was a fine morning. My master started off to Felbrigg Hall and Mr Baring went with him to shoot Sheringham. At night after dinner my master called for me and he told me that Mr Baring was very sorry for it and he had not been in such a passion for 20 years and that he was sorry for it and hoped that I would not think any more of it, which he acted like a gentleman there which I am happy to hear. My master let me out of the room this night without drinking for the first time since I first knew his honour, but that is all right at present.

Saturday 8 of September 1827

. . . My master sent me a note to say that if I found Mr Baring shooting on any part of my manor to say he is welcome. So he may, but not by me.'

The incident confirmed Banville's poor opinion of the Windhams, young Windham being labelled thereafter 'a shameful blackguard'. It also confirmed his good opinion of T. F. Buxton.

'Friday 31 of October 1827

. . . I may say that I have one of the best masters in this present age or I believe ever was in any age. I should like to write a volume about his goodness to me if my tongue could tell my pen what to write in his praise, also his noble family, but as I can't I will call on the Lord of all to do it for me.'

> To add to their other iniquities Banville believed the Windhams to be Sabbath-breakers and miserly into the bargain.

'Sunday 25 of November 1827

Tom Curtis the tailor of Cromer he tells me that this day the whole of Felbrigg Hall was playing billiards and that he saw a flight of wood pigeons alight under one of the beech trees. All loaded, the guns fired, 7 guns shot but no fowl did not fall to them as he says. They all was gone, only one bird and they could not kill it. What a thing for gentlemen to do the like, singing and playing cards of the Sabbath day in England.

Saturday 14 of November 1829

We went to Felbrigg. There were 7 guns . . . there were between 30 and 40 men and boys beating, nothing to eat or drink . . . for the beaters, what a shame to see a great estate man do so, it is a pity. I believe the half do not get one penny for beating for him, but a hare that is shot to pieces or a rabbit. Is not that a fine account of the great Admiral W.W. of Felbrigg Hall in Norfolk?'

> Events of the winter of 1827–8 were to bring Banville into contact with the younger branch of the Wyndham family. Shortly after his marriage to his cousin Maria Windham, George Wyndham, the owner of Cromer Hall, wished to have the house rebuilt for himself and his family. The Buxtons decided to rent Northrepps Hall from their relation Richard Gurney. It was rather small for their requirements, but it had the advantage of being close to Northrepps Cottage, the home of the Cottage Ladies. New shooting rights were also purchased at Weybourne and James Parsons was despatched thither as keeper. Larry and Sarah waited anxiously to hear how the changes would affect them.

'Friday 14 of December 1827

My master told me this day that he was to lose the Cromer [manor] and going to give the Runton manor to Barclay, and that he was going to lose [one of]

Northrepps Hall, drawn by Priscilla Buxton in 1834. The house was leased by T. F. Buxton from Anna Gurney's father, Richard Gurney, in 1828. Thomas Fowell died there in 1845 and his widow Hannah lived on there until her death in 1872.

his keepers, but that he would not part with me, that he was satisfied with me since I became his servant . . .

Monday 24 of December 1827
As I was at breakfast my wife asked me if I was sure that my master would send me to Northrepps, so I said if she would have patience the Lord would provide for her, and her answer was "I wish for 2 pails of water as it is washing day". I fetched her two at the same time.

Saturday 29 of December 1827
This day my master asked me if I would be willing to do anything for him at Northrepps Hall which I told him that I should do anything that lay in my power to do for him . . . This day all my fellow servants was saying that they did not like an Irishman, for what reason I cannot tell . . . I am sure they have no reason to assign for it but a bitterness that is in their minds

about the religion which, in my opinion, they know nothing about . . .

I believe there is more roguery in this county than any other in the known world by either rich or poor in this country or any other.'

The move took place in the coldest part of February 1828 at the tailend of the winter's shooting. There was snow on the 12th, but it did not lie. Ten woodcocks, five pheasants and some rabbits made up the last bag of the season on the 13th. Then, on the 14th, young Mr Wyndham came with his keepers to survey the game reserves.

'Thursday 14 of February 1828
. . . As the young Esquire was coming down the road he said to me "Larry, the more pheasants that you show me the better I will speak of you."

I said "I don't ask the Esquire for any favour, for if I would I would be disappointed." We went to a house in the town, got something to eat and drink.

All passed away, I am not able to say what joy that I feel at parting of the Cromer manor, but I will say that a few of the gentlemen of Cromer their goodness I shall never forget. I shall state their names as I am to leave them. Cromer, Mr Tucker and sons and all the family, Mr Sandford and son and the family, Mr G. Pank and son and family, Mr Press and his family. Runton,

Woodcock-shooting. the stacks of faggots were a normal feature in the woods.

Mr Revd. Parson Johnson and son, also Mr May and family and the most of the neighbours.

Sunday 17 of February 1828
This was a fine day. I went down to Cromer and I sat in the old pew, I suppose for the last time. I went with the servants to George Young's, had something to drink. I then returned home. I found my dear wife alone, but she was in such a temper. I am sitting up for to call the servants as they are all going away in the morning. A fine night, it is frost at present time.'

> The new occupants of Cromer Hall, being Wyndhams, soon met with Banville's disapproval.

'Saturday 12 of April 1828
. . . That Mrs G. Wyndham would gather all the fine firing in the woods and make her gardener burn it sooner than let the poor of Cromer have it to warm the poor little children's feet of a cold night. When Mrs Buxton lived at the same Hall she used to get faggots of furze cut and stacked up for them . . . also she gave all the rabbits that we used to get until the poor disputed about them because they all could not have good ones . . . Here is the different states between Mrs Buxton and Mrs. G Wyndham. She is a daughter of Admiral W.W. of Felbrigg Hall in Norfolk near Cromer. All the country knows him.'

> This period of the Wyndhams' occupation of Cromer Hall proved a tragic time for the family. In October 1829, the newly refurbished house was severely damaged by fire, and in February the following year, young George Wyndham, who had ridden through Cromer in triumph in the summer of 1826, died aged only twenty-four of 'a mysterious wasting illness'.

> If the Windhams fared badly in the diary, so also did some of the local clergy. Banville apparently had no qualms about repeating local gossip, some of it slanderous, some merely uncharitable. The most eminent local churchman was the Venerable Archdeacon Glover, MA, FRS, Rector of Southrepps and possibly the brother of the Buxtons' fierce governess, Miss Christiana Glover. In public he was a noted supporter of good causes, a school supervisor, a member of the Church Missionary Society and the Association for Saving the Lives of Shipwrecked Sailors. In private, according to Larry, he was not conspicuous for his generosity to the poor.

'Sunday 13 of August 1826

This was also a fine day. I went to church where I heard a good sermon taken from the 14, 13 – 14 of Saint Luke. One was for charity, the other was "When you make a feast invite the poor", but Mr Glover is to have a great Ball next Friday, but he will not have any poor man at it, for by all accounts he hate them . . .

Sunday 9 of September 1827

. . . Went to church, heard a good sermon preached by Mr Glover all about charity, but he have none of it. I suppose he would not give a penny to a poor man if it would save his life . . .'

> Larry frequently indulged in the popular sport of criticizing the preacher of the day. Archdeacon Glover read his sermons 'the same as a little boy would a ballad', Mr Hay of Northrepps 'preached like the whizzing of a bumblebee . . . all the one tone from the beginning to the ending', and poor Mr Clowes of Cromer had disciplinary problems.

'Sunday 15 of June 1828

At Cromer church all the people was talking the time of service. They pay but little regard to Mr Clowes.

Sunday 18 March 1827

In the morning went to church and heard Mr Clowes preach, but no singers which put me out and I afterwards learned that it was on account of 7 shillings that the man that played the organ got, put it all into his own pocket, which if all do attend funerals I think they ought to have a share of it, so on that account they did not sing . . .'

> Mr Clowes' evangelical curate, Mr Steel, did not escape criticism from Banville.

'Sunday 20 of April 1828

This day I went to church, heard Mr Steel preach a sermon and a very good one. He was at the beating of one of his own children the other day and swore that he would kill him and he frightened all that heard him.'

> The Reverend Benjamin Pulleyne of Upper Sheringham was the clergyman who had married Larry and Sarah in 1826. He was a good preacher and apparently a good headmaster at Holt Grammar School [now the famous Gresham's School] though rather over-addicted to the use of the cane. Banville calls him 'one of the

The tower of Cromer Church is 160 feet high and by far the tallest of any Norfolk parish church. Here, according to Larry, the Reverend Clowes preached, but few listened.

greatest Tories in these parts' and though he had a certain respect for him, he did not hesitate to commit to paper the scurrilous gossip that was being put about between 1830 and 1833.

'Sunday 25 of April 1830

I went to church. I heard a good sermon preached by Mr Pulleyne, but all do not speak well of him. Mr Warlowe says that when his daughter is at church his eyes is always upon the pew that she is in, but other times no eyes comes there. What a pity if it is true . . .

Sunday 6 of March 1831

There is a young woman of the name of Miss Warlowe in the workhouse that always comes a part of the way to meet Mr Pulleyne, also passes the house where [he] stops before and after service. I think she ought to have a little shame in her.

Wednesday 11 of July 1833

Here is a tale that Platten told me that he was told of Mr Pulleyne of Holt, he goes to preach at Barningham and stops for tea at Mr Partridge's, a farmer's, and takes away one of his daughters, keeps her out until 11 o'clock, sometimes later. What a shame! The servant man told Platten, that lives there.'

Banville proved fortunate in his domestic life. He remained fond of his wife despite their not-infrequent tiffs and Sarah, although she suffered much during pregnancy and childbirth, produced a family of eight healthy children. By contrast the families of the local gentry all suffered the sorrow of an early death. Admiral Windham lost his second son on active service in the navy in 1826, Lord Suffield an infant son in 1828. The Cromer Wyndhams had lost the young head of the family in 1830 and the Buxtons their beloved Harry in the same year. The Hoare family were not to escape for long. Their eldest son, Samuel, was a most promising young man. He took a brilliant degree in Classics at Cambridge in 1829 and was appointed Senior Wrangler in 1832. Some of the charming and humorous letters written to his mother from his school and university days still survive. From 1829, however, he was ominously troubled with a cough.

Young Sam Hoare was married at Bilney in September 1831 to Catherine Hankinson, the sister of his Cambridge friend, the

Reverend Tom Hankinson. The following year family letters record him bounding across Hampstead Heath shouting to his parents 'A girl! A girl!' to tell them of the birth of his daughter. But by the summer of 1833 he was seriously ill with consumption, and on 29 October he died.

'Saturday 1 of November 1833 [mistakenly put into 1832 by Banville] S. Hoare Esq. departed this life last Sunday morning. I trust it is well for him as the last word that he was heard to utter was "Lord I am thine." I trust it is well with him in the next life, I was sure it was well with him in this, but I must say a nice young man he was as a master as far as I know of him, and I know him since a child, so I hope he got his reward as it is given to all in the next world. There is a great mourning for him in this world by his dear parents.

Robert Tooker also departed this life the same morning, but it is thought nothing of by the grand folks, but what a loss to his dear wife and his dear 4 little ones to be left to the mercy of the parish, which is a poor thing for anyone at this time of the enlightened age as they call it. He was a yard man at Mrs. Upcher's for a long time, liked by all that had any dealings with him.'

> There was no funeral oration for Robert Tooker, but family and servants all gathered at Northrepps Hall to hear an address from Joseph John Gurney on the subject of young Sam Hoare.

'Sunday 2 of November 1833
I met James Parsons at the Hall and he drove me over to Northrepps Hall. The call was to hear Joe John Gurney Esq. of Earlham Hall to speak of Samuel Hoare Esq., a fine man indeed he is to speak to any hearers. There were 72 in the room of all sorts both ladies as well as gentlemen. They were a set of fine-looking people altogether . . . The sea run mountains high this day and night. We got all our hearts could wish for at the hall in regard of refreshment.'

> Although Banville clearly felt both loyalty and affection for the Buxtons, and for their relations and friends the Hoares and Upchers, his attitude to them has some of the detachment that arises from the class division and from the total separation of their social lives. There was always a part of his mind which felt free to criticize them as people and to convey this criticism to the pages of a diary which he hoped would one day be read by the general public.

In his attitude to the neighbouring families such as the Wyndhams and Lord Suffield, Larry openly reflected the popular prejudices of his neighbours. The heads of the families at Felbrigg and Gunton both died within a short time of each other. Admiral Windham died in January 1833. His neighbour, Lord Suffield, was tragically killed in a riding accident in 1835, and the contrast between the two men in popular memory was recorded in a strange incident the following year.

'Monday 16 of May 1836

This day I heard a queer story of the young people at Roughton. Three of them fell into a trance for a good many hours. They says how that they went to the both places in the next world. They says that they saw men that was dead and tells the people that Lord Suffield is in the good place and that Admiral Windham of Felbrigg Hall is in the bad place. What a thing for these poor creatures to report to other deluded creatures . . .'

Chapter Eight

——————⌘——————

THE MOVE TO
SHERINGHAM

1828–30

When George Wyndham moved into Cromer Hall in February
1828 Larry said farewell to Cromer and presumably moved with
the Buxtons to Northrepps. He must have had temporary lodgings
there for about a year, during which time his wife, Sarah, gave
birth to a daughter. Then, in February 1829, arrangements were
made for the Banvilles to move into Sheringham Lodge, which had
previously been occupied by George Ridout and his family.

Larry later gave this description of his new home.

'On the north side of the Cromer road at the cross ways to Beckham and Bodham, also to Sheringham, just 4½ miles from Holt, 1 from West Beckham, 2
from Lower Sheringham, then it is 5½ miles from Cromer, a fine road for a ride
or a drive in the summer season. This lodge is all covered with jenny to the very
top of it. There is . . . on its top . . . a look-out as a deal of the quality from all
parts comes to it . . . also the grand room, I believe they call it the front room
. . . is a round one with the front a window which gives it a grand appearance,
but this is all, for nothing else is in its beauty to be spoken of as it is the worst
place for water in the whole town and to my cost I know it. Often after hunting
all day I had to go for water before I could feed a dog. What a place to stick a
keeper in! I am ashamed to say this that I often cursed them that built it. The
old saying is "Cursed is the house that Jack built".'

The house that Banville cursed was designed by Humphry Repton
and built in 1811 when he was preparing plans for Sheringham Hall.
A small painting of it by Repton survives. It was burned down at the
turn of this century and the Lodge which now stands on the site was
built in 1904 on very much the same plan as the original except that the
roof was tiled not thatched and had no look-out point.

WHERE KILLED. Sheringham	WHEN.	GROUSE. stoto	PART-RIDGE. Wesel	PHEA-SANT. hawk	WOOD-COCK. fays	SNIPE. Cats	WILD FOWL, &c. Iguin	HARE. k.e	RABBIT. hedge	NUMBER OF GUNS.	TOTAL EACH DAY and WEEK.
	Monday, 1829	1	25	22	4	17	54	954	11		1001
	Tuesday, 1830	9	19	10	5	9	72	1352	35		1401
	Wednesday 1831	12	47	9	1	13	10	506	17		613
	Thursday, 1832	0	11	20	2	9	-	565	13		610
	Friday, 1833	12	44	9	1	13	-	513	17		600
	Saturday, 1834	8	30	~	3	11	-	339	43		444
	TOTAL....	45	176	70	16	72	136	4200	136		4260

Sporting Occurrences, Engagements, &c.—Memorandum of Game, how disposed of by Gamekeeper, &c. &c.

Larry's Game Book, 1829–34. He used a standard game book, but changed the species in the columns. The entries are stoats (spelt stotes), weasels, hawks, jays, cats, squirrels, rats and hedgehogs. It is surprising to see squirrels, as they must have been red squirrels. Hawks are now protected.

The move to Sheringham brought Larry into more frequent contact with the Upcher family who lived at Sheringham. Charlotte Upcher was a handsome widow with several daughters and three sons approaching manhood. She was a generous lady both publicly and privately. In addition to being the benefactress of the Sheringham life-boat, she supported a free school in the town and frequently gave free meals to the poor at festival times. There was always good food to be had at Sheringham Hall and she provided by far the best meals for the shooting gentlemen, as the diary shows.

'Wednesday 4 of October 1826
I joined them at [Beeston] bog – they shot snipes well. The game that was bagged is partridges 18, pheasants 6 . . . 1 landrail, 17 snipes, 1 hare, 3 rabbits. This day it was so hot that it was very hard for us to walk the heath as the brakes was so thick on them, but it was not any great fatigue to me. I must say that Mrs Upcher sent us a good lunch, the same as a good dinner. I wish all in this county had as good. There were plenty of beef of the best. I wished that Mrs Upcher might ne'er want a cow or a calf for sending us such a piece of beef. My master was well pleased with me for saying so. My

[111]

master cut a pear and told me to carry one half of it on a very small penknife
. . . I told his honour that it was very tempting which he cut it and gave me
a lump of it as he done with his lordship's lunch. Mrs Upcher came home
with us this night.

Tuesday 21 of July 1829
. . . I dined at Mrs. Upcher's along with a company of men. Mrs Upcher was
dressed very neat with black silk, all her arms and neck was naked . . .

Sunday 25 of September 1831
. . . I saw 184 at dinner at Mrs Upcher's school room . . . a day of feast I
believe it was, more than it was a day of prayer with a good many that was
at the feast. They say rest, but there were no rest there this day. It was a day
of hard work for all the servants. Mrs Upcher and 2 of her daughters waited
as well as my friend Mr Pulleyne, the clergyman of the parish, and a lady
friend of his that came with him.'

> Banville had his reservations about Mrs Upcher. She was some-
> times overbearing and he suspected that she had a more than
> neighbourly affection for his master.

'Thursday 28 of November 1826
This morning we started off to Sheringham in the phaeton . . . They shot
pretty fair . . . We were favoured with Mrs Upcher's company for a good
while. She amused herself by putting the wadding in the gun for my master
and the caps on the tubes which was very handsome to see . . .

Monday 5 of December 1826
. . . It turned to heavy wet this day in the evening. We were forced to wait
for the game. Mrs Upcher and my master walked on before us – a man cannot
be hanged for thinking, but he can for speaking. I will not speak . . .

Monday 4 of January 1830
. . . Mrs Buxton wrote a note to say that my master would shoot with me
tomorrow if the day would allow. Mrs Upcher sent up for the note to see

---

'The old Cromer lighthouse', a watercolour by an unknown artist. An inscription on the
back reads 'Cromer Lighthouse was dismantled in 1834 . . . The tower stood for more than
32 years afterwards and went down the cliff on a day in November 1866.'

A shooting party at Felbrigg. William Windham (né Lukin) with his three brothers in
front of Felbrigg Parsonage, later known as Felbrigg Cottage, which was their home before
1824. The keeper fastens his master's gaiters. Artist unknown.

what was in it. I think what a lady would think of a servant to do such a thing, but anything is good enough for a servant . . . She done it before at the time I was a single man in Sheringham, she opened a letter of mine.

Monday 21 of November 1831
I sent to Mrs Upcher for 2 pheasants, 2 woodcocks . . . The 2 pheasants came but the woodcocks did not come. At my arrival in Northrepps Mrs Upcher had them there which my worthy master gave them to her for her dear father . . . I make no doubt but that was why she kept them back which it was very kind of him to do so. She is a very nice lady if a man do not care what they say.

Monday 25 of November 1832
. . . I settled the game account with Mrs Upcher. She says she is going out for a few days, so is my master . . . It is all right with the rich whatever they do . . .'

> The scandalous suggestion contained in this entry has been scored out in the manuscript diary, whether by Larry himself, or by another hand we shall probably never know.
>
> Despite his suspicions about Mrs Upcher, Banville did not like to see her taken advantage of by her estate employees.

'Friday 4 of March 1831
This morning I took the liberty of calling on Mrs Upcher to tell her that I should like very much if her ladyship would tell her master carpenter to do that covert that is at the oak woods. She was quite surprised it wasn't done, but she sent for him and his answer was he had no timber and it is only little wonder for him not to have it as he sells all and cuts it up for firing. All is very well if the estate affairs is looked to first . . . It will be seen when it will be too late for the heir, H. Upcher Esq.

'The lodge, Sheringham Hall' by Humphry Repton. Built as a keeper's house at the entrance to the south drive of Sheringham Hall, it was occupied successively by the Ridouts and the Banvilles during the period of the diaries. It was burned down at the turn of the century and the present lodge was built in 1904 to a similar plan, but without the thatch.

A general view of Sheringham Bower, now known as Sheringham Hall. Begun in 1813, the house which Humphry Repton designed was not completed until much later, owing to the tragic early death in 1819 of its founder, Abbot Upcher. His widow, Charlotte, and their six children lived on in the old house, and the Bower was only occupied when Henry Ramey Upcher was married in 1838.

Saturday 20 of July 1831
This day I went to Mrs Upcher's harvest men and they were cutting the
wheat right against the wind, but they will cut any way for the sake of a
rabbit and they were very sorry for me to say a word to them . . . Mrs Upcher
have a steward and he is a stupid ass for his mistress. I have seen 14 men
and 3 or perhaps 6 boys running through her barley for a rabbit. That is not
the way that I should do if I was her man . . . Let 14 men run through
standing barley for 10 or 12 minutes, see what they will spoil. But it is all
right with them if they get a rabbit and spoil 2 or 3 bushels of Mrs Upcher's
corn . . . It is a pity to do so on a widow, but it will fall on their heads for
so doing, for cursed is he that defraud a widow.'

> Banville acted as keeper at Sheringham from 1829 until 1835.
> Thomas Fowell and Sam Hoare frequently shot there, but quite
> often it was the Upcher boys, Harry, Abbot and Arthur who went
> out with Larry. They seem to have been likeable young men,
> though sometimes inclined to forget that Larry, like other men,
> needed food and drink to keep him going. The two younger boys,
> both clergymen in later life, got Larry into trouble at the beginning
> of the 1829 season.

'Monday 7 of September 1829
This day I was out with Mr Abbot Upcher and Mr Arthur Upcher, nice
young gentlemen, but I must say that Abbot is as wild as any young willock
[guillemot] that e'er was on the sea coast, but a good-natured young man.
They killed 14 partridges, 4 were old ones. At the close of the day . . . Mrs
Upcher came to me and asked me who gave them leave to shoot. I said that
I thought that they had got leave to do so or that they would not have done
it, but she told me that I ought to have asked her about it, but I ask anyone
in my way of life if there are anyone in this country would think any other
thing but they got leave when they ordered me to be down before breakfast,
and they were out also from prayers and breakfast, but I think nothing about
it, as my master I make no doubt will think nothing about it . . . If anyone
in my station of life ever see this they will think it a queer story of Mrs
Upcher.'

> Larry had some complaints to make about later winter expeditions
> with the two younger boys.

'Saturday 18 of December 1830
This was a day of storm and hail. I went down to Weybourne with the 2

young gentlemen . . . They shot in the fields, killed 6 partridges. The wind and hail was so much I hardly could see 100 yards before my nose. They wanted lunch. James went for it – he brought all sausage rolls and hot brandy and water . . . At my arrival to Mrs Upcher's at night I was tired enough and the 2 Mr Upchers did not as much as ask me to eat or drink a drop. I ate 4 potatoes and a drop of beer. I went home . . .

Saturday 19 of November 1831
This morning I got my breakfast at an early hour. I done all that I had to do. I then went to Mrs Upcher's. Then we drove off to Blakeney and it was a cold morning. We all got a small glass of brandy and water. We started off to the muds with a small drop of brandy in a bottle. We got a pair of boots and stockings for Mr Arthur Upcher from the landlord of the house. We were so hungry that we begged a few biscuits of a man aboard of a vessel at the harbour. He [Mr Upcher] ne'er offered to pay for what we had or got a drop to drink and at my arrival home did not get as much as a drop of his beer, but he ought to go sporting by himself for the time to come to serve a dog so . . .'

Life as a keeper at Sheringham was very little different from Larry's previous existence. One day was very much like another, but there were highlights and days of drama recorded with relish in the pages of the diary.
   In November 1829 Mrs Upcher gave Larry some news of his old master Llewellyn Lloyd which clearly excited him. He was to meet Mr Lloyd at Holt the following Tuesday and they were to shoot together at Sheringham.

'Saturday 7 of November 1829
I cannot tell my feelings. At the same time I am happy to hear he is coming to see me to this part of the globe.

Tuesday 10 of November 1829
This was a stormy day . . . It turned to heavy wet at half past 4 o'clock. It fell in as great torrents as I ever saw in all my life. I was afraid that it would disappoint me of seeing my old master this night, but at 9 o'clock it rise up as fine a night as anyone ever saw. I then started off with Mrs Upcher's horse and cart to Holt. I fed the horse. He just fed and at the same time the coach

came in and I spoke to his honour and he shook hands with me and [said] "I like to shake hands with an honest man", which all that heard him was laughing at a gentleman talking to me in that manner. I . . . put the horse in and drove home to Mrs Upcher's and there I got plenty of everything that my heart could wish for. I then took his gun and started off for home at 1 o'clock. My master confined me to the top of the heath. I am sure that I will not get good shooting.

Wednesday 11 of November 1829
This was a morning I was sorry for, to go to my old master and confine him to where I am sure there will be no sport for him. I was not down until late in the morning. He and I then walked through the streets of Sheringham. All was willing to see Larry's old master. In the course of the day he bagged 17 partridges, 2 woodcocks – he killed them with a double shot . . . I then drove off to Northrepps where I had the honour to drink to my old master's good health with my master's good wine at Northrepps . . . My master was in the best of humour and spirits.'

The following January on a stormy day near the end of the game season there was a shooting expedition that came near to ending in tragedy.

'Monday 11 of January 1830
This morning my young master [probably Harry Buxton] and the 3 Mr Upchers and I went out to shoot. The day was a stormy one. I went to the cliff where Summers offered me a piece of a large eel which I accepted of it. Mr H. Upcher lit a cigar with my gun then, to cut my story short, the lunch made its appearance and came down between the new barn and the cliff in the corner of the 30 acres . . . It was as follows – a beef steak pudding and bread and cheese, plenty of drink of wine and water. I hardly ever saw Mr H. Upcher in such humour. He told us that we all might go down to Lower Sheringham and all get as drunk as beasts after lunch. I lit a match with my gun and he let it out. With laughter I lit another and . . . which was a very awful thing for me [to do] . . . I put a little powder into my gun to school it as I was willing not to have it hang fire. The powder horn took fire and away it went which made such a crack that I thought my hand was off, but I was happy to say it was only little hurt, but at the same time the powder caught Mr Harry Upcher's eyes. He fell to the ground. When I recovered my paw from the horn the first thing was to see what was the matter. I believe they cried out "Mr Upcher is killed!". I went to him and asked him what was the

matter. He said "You shot me". I made him let me look at his face. I cried out "Let us start forth". The others said "Send for the carriage". I said not, but to go home and steal the mare out and go for the doctor. We called at Shore's house and got a little water, washed his face and eyes, then sent off to the house to let them know what had happened. I came to the laundry and there the mother and 4 ladies met us. At the same time my heart failed me, for I dare not go to the house. I made the best of my way home where I clapped tow and sweet oil on my hand and tied it up. My heart and nerves was all cold. Mrs Upcher sent for me to go down to the house [where] the Dr Earle was come. That made me feel ten times worse than before. I went down, sat in the nursery where the ladies all used me well. They made me tea. My honoured master came from Northrepps in about twenty minutes, I believe it was under . . . he thought we were half killed. There were 7 of us in the whole. There were others more torn than Mr Upcher, but he had the cigar in his mouth. By that means I believe it caught him. There were about ¼lb of powder in the horn. It was a tin one which was well for Poor Larry . . .

Tuesday 12 of January 1831
This day I went to see Mr Upcher, he was as merry as anyone could wish for . . .

. . . At present my hand is easy.

Friday 15 of January 1831
. . . I am happy to say that Mr Upcher is getting better. He had 12 leeches all round his eyes. My hand is almost well, it is neither one thing nor the other.'

Despite the fact that Banville had a good situation with benevolent masters whom he took satisfaction in serving well, he clearly missed Ireland and his Irish family at times. In the summer of 1830 he took steps to obtain some news from his Irish home. At the same time he hoped to get some good dogs for Mr Buxton and incidentally to provide Mrs Upcher's free school with a new, if somewhat reluctant, pupil.

In April he sent £5 over to Ireland to pay for his brother Paddy to visit him in Norfolk and to bring with him two Irish setter pups. On an evening in June, when Larry was relaxing and nursing a sore heel after a hard day shooting sparrows with the Upcher boys, the young traveller arrived.

'Wednesday 16 of June 1830
I was at home going to take some supper with my wife and my dear brother

Paddy made his appearance at my cottage, but to my great surprise he did not bring the setters with him, but for all that I am happy that he came to see me and my dear wife and 2 children in this part, but I must say that I should [have] liked to see the pups with him . . .'

> Larry was given permission to employ Paddy as his assistant if he wished, but he decided not to do so, no doubt fearing the jealousy of the many unemployed local men. However, he took his brother out with him to ferret rabbits and shoot sparrows, he gave him crabs to eat which he liked, and lobsters which he did not. Then, on Sunday, he sent him to Mrs Upcher's school. We do not know how old Paddy was, but his brother evidently felt that a little schooling would not go amiss.

'Sunday 20 of June 1830
. . . I sent my brother Paddy to Mrs Upcher's school and the boys [began] to make game of him [so] he went and stopped at the public house for near 4 hours which I did not like by no means as it was but last Wednesday he came to this country and . . . I think he ought to [have] stopped with me and my wife and two children.'

> The following day they went to Aldborough Fair.

'Monday 21 of June 1830
. . . I took my brother, of course, my wife and old Mrs Pegg of Sheringham. The ground was very wet, so it was that my wife was forced to buy a pair of pattens to keep her feet out of the mud. The people said it was a very bad fair . . .'

> As the days of Paddy's visit passed, it became clear that, given the choice, he preferred drinking to schooling.

'Sunday 5 of July 1830
This day I thought my dear brother Paddy was at Mrs Upcher's school, but he was at the public house which I did not like by no means.

Saturday 17 of July 1830
. . . my brother is like a dead man in the bed. He drank something at Cromer and it disagreed with him . . .'

> It was perhaps with some relief that Larry saw his brother off to the 'Land of the Potatoes' at the beginning of August.

'Tuesday 3 of August 1830
I took farewell of my brother Pat this night. He started off by the carriage to Norwich. My wife and 2 children was sorry for his departure . . .'

Chapter Nine

BUXTON FAMILY
FORTUNES

1828–36

By the time the Buxtons moved into Northrepps Hall in 1828 T. F. Buxton was well on the way to recovery from a slight stroke he had suffered in May of the previous year. While he was convalescing Banville was often out shooting with Sam Hoare alone. Sam was an energetic man, described by Larry as 'always in a bustle'. Unfortunately, despite his obvious enthusiasm, he was a poor shot. Larry frequently tells his readers that Mr Hoare 'shot as usual bad', and on one occasion, after a day of 'great misery', he writes,

'In truth I believe his gun is the best in the county, or at least it is able to kill birds in style if it is held straight.'

It says much for his kindly good humour that, despite his failure to reach the required standard of accuracy with the gun, Larry continued to like and respect him and to enjoy his company, as he clearly did one autumn day.

'Saturday 20 of September 1828
This was a fine day, I got breakfast at Mr S. Hoare's and then we got into a boat, sailed away to Lower Sheringham, then to Weybourne, from that to Salthouse. There we met James Parsons and then he ordered us to go to Cley and there we would get good sport, but it was poor sport, for all the game that was shot was 9 head. I bagged 5 of them to my own gun and one of them was a snipe . . . I arrived home to Cromer after 4 hours sailing and rowing. I got my dinner at Mr S. Hoare's, one fish which was very good. It is past 9 o'clock. I am tired enough of my day's sport. I believe Mr S.H. Esq. is the same. I was very cold on the water all the way. On our way to Weybourne I saw a man on the cliff. I fired off my gun to alarm him as we thought it to be James Parsons, [but] a man of Lower Sheringham said that

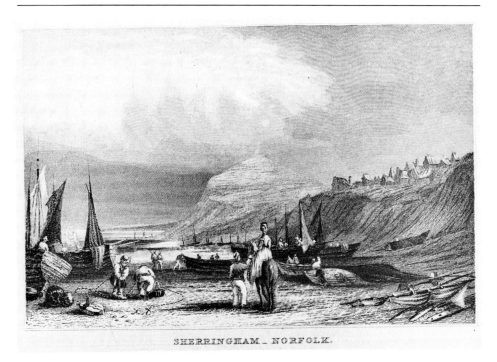

SHERRINGHAM — NORFOLK.

A view of Lower Sheringham beach. Fishing was the chief occupation of the people at
this end of the town.

we shot at him and swore that he would come and swim to the boat and let
all of us into the sea. What would 5 guns be at while he and his partner
would do that? I should let shot into the King to save myself . . . I am sure
I would not stop for a fisherman of Lower Sheringham . . . The day was
spent with great mirth.'

> Although, for a time, Buxton went out shooting less frequently
> Larry still saw much of him and his surviving children: Priscilla,
> Edward, Harry, Richenda, Fowell and Charles. Of all the children
> Banville's favourite was Harry. Back in May 1826 he had written,

'This was a fine day. My young master Harry, the flower of my master's
family, came to me at 12 o'clock. He walked up to Burnt Hills, fired a few
shots at small birds, killed none. He shot 3 rooks with one shot – he was well
pleased, he gave me one and ordered the other two to be dressed for his
dinner the next day. I skinned the three for him as I could shoot one at any
time for myself. This act of kindness shows his good and tender heart.'

Harry was a keen sportsman and an enthusiastic collector of birdskins and Larry was always glad to be able to find new skins for his collection. However, there were worries about Harry's health and when his elder brother, Edward, was sent away to school at Brighton, Harry stayed at home, receiving instruction from the Reverend and Miss Clowes during the week, and from the Cottage ladies at week-ends. Sarah Buxton wrote in 1827, 'Shakespeare, history and biography employed our Saturdays, and our Sundays were filled with a succession of active and religious duties'.

In November 1828 Harry himself began to keep a journal and occasionally we can set his account of the day beside Larry's own. On Monday 1 December 1828 Banville wrote,

'The wind wheeled out to the north-eastward which is a bad wind for shipping on this coast. It turned a heavy storm, drove a ship ashore at Cromer, all hands saved.'

On the same day Harry wrote in his journal,

'Edmund [his cousin] and I were sitting at work when the wind rattled round the corner tremendously, and Mr Clowes told us to go and see what was to be seen. The wind was so high from the north-east that I was blown down in the churchyard. When we arrived on the cliff we discovered a vessel about a mile and a half from land, in the greatest danger. The wind was tremendous, the sea getting up rapidly. I went back to Colne House, mounted my pony, and rode up to Northrepps to tell Cousin Anna and my father, and as I was going I saw the ship coming in at a terrible rate. Cousin Anna went off to Sidestrand, and my father to Cromer. When I arrived there the ship was ashore, by the gangway. The crew (three men and a boy) were ashore safe. Hundreds of oranges were floating about, and men and boys up to their shoulders in the sea to get them. It was a most curious scene'.

During 1829 Harry's health deteriorated and he was only occasionally out with Banville.

'Monday 2 of February 1829
... Master H. Buxton and I walked to the sea shore. I walked near the water and he near the cliff and I turned the gulls to him, he shot 7. At Hungry Hills saw 3 snipes – got none. I shot one water hen. Mr H. was very tired, I must say that I was not free myself.'

[121]

On Tuesday evening, 29 September 1829, Harry began to cough blood, confirming the worst fears of his family. 'A death stroke, I knew it to be', wrote his mother, 'and it is impossible to say what a night of suffering I passed'. Thomas Fowell lay beside Harry on his bed that night and read to him till he fell asleep. The next day Banville records

'I saw Ridout. He came to settle with my master, but his son, Harry, is too unwell to speak about anything.'

And a month later –

'Monday 26 of October 1829
This morning I started off to Northrepps. I saw my worthy young master, H. Buxton, but not as well as I could wish to see him if it was the Lord's will, but His will be done to us all.'

The previous evening Harry had made the last entry in his own journal.

'The thought occurs to me whether I shall ever see October 25, 1830; whether I shall be on earth, or gone to stand before the Tribunal of Jehovah . . . I often feel as if I should not live long, therefore let me work while it is day, for the night cometh when no man can work.'

Various changes of air were tried during the following year, but to no effect, and in August 1830 he returned to Norfolk for the last time.

'Monday 30 of August 1830
This day I saw master H.B. whom I daily grieve for his ills, but I hope he is in favour with the Saviour of the world is my constant prayer. He was my sincere friend. I told him about the lightning and also about me seeing a woodcock, but he ne'er smiled which was a grief to me to see him in that state that nothing can be done for him.'

By October, Harry was being taken about Northrepps Hall in a wheelchair, and on 18 November 1830 he died. It can hardly be coincidence that at this point in Banville's diary two pages, covering the days from 12 to 23 November, have been torn out. Whether Banville himself, re-reading his diary in old age, found the memories it aroused too painful and removed the pages of his own accord, or whether Charles Buxton removed them during his researches into the life of his father, we shall probably never know. The only further reference to Harry Buxton is as follows –

'Wednesday 24 of November 1830
His height was six foot one inch. He departed this life on 18 of this month.
They all says there were nothing only the skin and bones together. I did not
see him after death.'

Harry Buxton was buried in Overstrand Church where there is a
memorial tablet to him and to the other Buxton children who died
much earlier.

The Buxtons bore their sufferings with quite extraordinary
patience and resignation, but even Thomas Fowell occasionally
gave way to melancholy. On 30 January 1831 he wrote

'I feel this morning more than usual dejection, partly occasioned
perhaps by the prospect of leaving this quiet place on Tuesday
next, and plunging once more into the distracting cares and
hurries of Parliament and business; but still more by a most
painful picture which suddenly burst upon me yesterday. I took
the boys, Edward, Edmund, and the two Upchers, to shoot on
the Warren Hills opposite the coast. The ground was covered
with snow, the sea was dark and fretful. I went along the lower
side, and turned up one of the most distant hillocks, and there
I placed myself. And then in a moment a picture burst upon me,
which made this one of the most melancholy moments of the last
melancholy year. On that same hillock about the same day two
years back, I stood. Nature seemed as if she had not changed.
The same surface of white beneath my feet, the sea bearing the
same blackening aspect, the gamekeepers and dogs in the same
hollow, and the boys exhibiting the same eagerness; all was the
same with one sorrowful exception. Dearest Harry was nearest
to me on the former occasion; his quick eye perceived a wild
duck sailing near the sea, and we observed it alighting in a pond
near the farm below us. I sent him, full of life and alacrity as he
was, to secure the bird, while I stood and watched his ma-
noeuvres to get within shot unobserved. Then again his exulting
return with the bird in his hand, and the pleasure I felt at his
pleasure – and now I could see nothing but the churchyard where
his bones repose. Dear fellow! How large a portion of my hope
and joy lies there: how has the world changed with me since that
hour! But there is this comfort, if we are left to sad recollections
he is gone to eternal security and peace.'

The Buxtons' private tragedy was to be followed very closely by a serious outbreak of violence amongst the distressed Norfolk labourers. This was a terrible time for the poor. There was widespread unemployment in town and country. The cloth trade was badly affected by the competition from the newly mechanized mills of Yorkshire and Lancashire. Some hand-weavers were out of work and others had been forced to accept reduced wages. The cost of bread and beer was kept artificially high by the operation of the Corn Laws and the Malt Tax. Farm labourers who had work were paid pitifully low wages, and the introduction of threshing machines on some farms had deprived the men of the extra harvest money that they had come to rely upon. Some small farmers were forced to give up their land as a result of the enclosures still being carried out in some Norfolk parishes; they had to join the ranks of the common farm labourers. Larry wrote –

'In this country they will not allow the poor sort of people any land to live on, only give it in large farms and make one man live on the work of 5 or 6 the same as the owners of the slaves abroad, but what end will become of these rich men that will feed their dogs a deal better than they feed the poor . . . Bread and water is chiefly their food in this town of Cromer.'

Several contributors to the *Norwich Mercury* at this time attempted to isolate the root causes of the trouble. One said the cause was the 'separation of the labourers from the soil . . . deprivation of the small patches of land formerly attached to cottages, and in the absorption of small farms into large'. Another put it down to the 'overwhelming burden of taxation' and the fact that Parliament was not elected 'by the people at large'. The magistrates, meanwhile, were worried by the increasing crime rate. Colonel Wodehouse declared in January 1829 that 'persons could not sleep safe in their beds'. Lord Suffield put it down to the 'high price of provisions and the operation of the Game Laws'. Colonel Harvey 'had no hesitation in declaring his conviction that the increase of crime arose mainly from the totally inadequate earnings of the agricultural labourer, who was not paid as he ought to be'.

The winter of 1829–30 had been a hard one and benevolent gentry and clergy had done what they could to alleviate the distress of poor families by distributions of soup, coals and blankets. A few landlords actually reduced their rents. Lord Suffield brought forward a plan to give all labourers a patch of land, but it was all too little and too late. In the autumn of 1830 the distress and discontent of the poor began to erupt into violence.

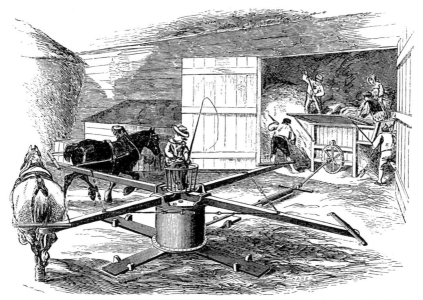

A horse-powered threshing machine. Threshing with wooden flails had previously kept men in work during the winter months. The introduction of horse-powered machines like this on many larger farms after 1815 further reduced the earnings of already under-paid labourers.

Stack-burning in Kent. The troubles of 1830 began in Kent before spreading to East Anglia.

Melton Constable *in Norfolk, the Seat of Sir Edw.ᵈ Astley Bar.ᵗ*

Melton Constable Hall, which was threatened by rioters during the agricultural troubles of 1830. Its owner, Sir Edward Astley, had stones thrown at him by a mob of over five hundred men at Reepham.

The trouble began in Kent and quickly spread to Norfolk where the violence took three forms: burning of stacks, breaking of threshing machines and the assembling of armed mobs to extract higher wages under threat of violence. The *Norfolk Chronicle* for 20 November reported stack-burning at Briston and the destruction of threshing machines at Cromer and Paston. The *Norwich Mercury* for 27 November spoke of 'various acts of outrage which have for the last few days affrighted, afflicted and disgraced the county of Norfolk'. Stacks had been burnt at Thorpe, Caister and Beeston Regis. More threshing machines had been broken up at Briston, Hindolveston, Cawston, Oulton, Blickling, Thurning and Hockering. Archdeacon Glover's house at Southrepps had been attacked and Melton Hall threatened by rioters. Troops were called out to Holt and North Walsham, and when eleven arrests were made at Briston, members of the hunt at North Elmham were summoned to escort them to Norwich lest they should be rescued by the mob.

WE the undersigned Magistrates acting in and for the Hundred of Gallow, in the County of Norfolk, do promise to use our utmost Endeavours and Influence we may possess, to prevail upon the Occupiers of Land in the said Hundred,

To discontinue the use of Thrashing Machines, and to take them to pieces.

Dated this 29th. day of November, 1830.

CHAS. TOWNSHEND.
ROBERT NORRIS.
EDW. MARSHAM.

STEWARDSON AND SON, PRINTERS, FAKENHAM.

A notice from the magistrates for the Hundred of Gallow, urging the destruction of threshing machines.

Banville was distressed by what he heard and saw, hating the lawless violence but hating also the harshness of the law.

'Tuesday 23 of November 1830

. . . The country is in the devil of a row. There were a cat sent to the Duke of Wellington with its head off and the foot and tail and a note to say that is the way they would serve his grace. They are burning stock of all sorts in this country. It is a shame . . .

[127]

Friday 26 of November 1830

... My master came about 1 o'clock, but was soon overtaken by Mr Playford of Sidestrand, for all the men was got together ... My master started off with him. I hardly ever saw a man in such a fright. A good gale of wind from the eastward. All the boatmen is gone to different parts of the country. Everyone is on the alert. I fear that hanging and transporting will follow this in short.

Saturday 27 of November 1830

The mob came to my master's house yesterday. Previous to their arrival a farmer in the town run to my master and said "They are coming, and have [care] sir, go armed to meet them." "Well, so I will," said he, called 3 of his dear children, Miss Buxton and Fowell Buxton and Master Charles Buxton, got them by the hands and said "Here I am, well armed." [He] met the men and they asked his honour what was to be done and he [said] to a couple of men that had some two sticks, "Give me those sticks". So they did. He gave one to each of his sons and said, "They have the staffs and I charge them with the whole of you". They all laughed at the joke and started [away]. The Archdeacon put 4 of them to prison at Southrepps, but they are always ready for anything of the kind, the parsons I mean, in any part. A great gale of wind.

Tuesday 30 of November 1830

This morning I went off to Northrepps Hall. My master was the most of the day at Gunton Hall with the magistrates and his Lordship [Lord Suffield]. All is now with my honoured masters – it is troublous times for all.

Friday 3 of December 1830

... There were a man of the name of James Hand taken away from Sheringham this day for breaking Bidewell's threshing machine. If all was of my mind they should take the whole, they have taken 2 or 3 more of the neighbours in the neighbourhood.'

The harvest was probably the most important event in the rural year. Men, women and children shared the toil and the excitement. Artist unknown.

'Woodcock' by Archibald Thorburn. The sand dunes of North Norfolk are often the first landfall for woodcock after their tiring flight across the North Sea from Scandinavia or Holland. Here two recent arrivals rest in the marram grass.

The troubles spread during the following week. Taverham paper mills were attacked and Sir Jacob Astley was pelted with stones at Reepham where several hundred men gathered demanding 'more work and a larger loaf'. The Foulsham area became infected, so did the coastal villages from Blakeney to Kelling. Three farmers at Bodham received letters threatening violence if they did not raise their men's wages to 2s. 3d. a week.

The authorities, on the whole, acted with moderation. Many farmers gave in to the demand for higher wages and, on the advice of the magistrates, laid aside their threshing machines for the time being. The Lord Lieutenant asked the magistrates to appoint special constables for each parish who were to call meetings to discuss the complaints of the poor. Nevertheless, many arrests were made and the law-breakers had to be punished. Some two hundred and ten cases came before the January Sessions in Norwich, of which seventy-seven were acquitted. Sixty-seven men were found guilty of machine-breaking and nine of them were sentenced to transportation, one of them for fourteen years. The others were given prison sentences ranging from two weeks to two years. Twenty-seven were found guilty of riot with sentences from one week to two and a half years in prison, and thirty-four were convicted of petty larceny. Nine cases were sent to a higher court, three capital cases of machine-breaking and six cases of arson.

By January the county was quiet again with nothing more alarming than the appearance of the northern lights recorded by Banville on 10 January 1831. While many Norfolk households struggled through the winter without their menfolk, others turned their thoughts to a new life elsewhere.

'Monday 28 of March 1831
There did 12 men and women and children start from Lower Sheringham for America. There is one have a famous offer to start. His passage is paid for himself and his wife and to have six shillings and three pence per day if all do be well with him, and if the country will not agree with him or his wife, they are to be paid back again, so it is the finest offer that I ever heard of, but in my mind he is not fit to undertake such a journey . . .'

'Abbot Upcher, son of Charlotte Upcher' by George Richmond. Two of Charlotte's sons, Abbot and Arthur, entered the church.

It had been a melancholy season and Larry had worries of his own, for Sarah was approaching the end of her third pregnancy. With the spring the baby arrived.

'Tuesday 15 of March 1831

This morning I was up at [an] early hour. I went down into town, I sent the women up to my wife. I then started off to Cromer for Mr Earle junior [the doctor]. At 11½ after a young daughter came to the world for me. The doctor stopped for near 2 hours with my wife . . . My dear wife was so ill that we all thought it was all up with her. The first word that she spoke to me was "I am dying" . . . My brother-in-law Leonard Lown went to Cromer in about 15 or 18 minutes without a saddle for the doctor. My other brother-in-law went to bed. In a few minutes the old Dr Earle came, but I thank God the turn was in my favour. The Lord was pleased to spare her for me and my dear little children . . .'

A week later young Samuel Banville was taken to school.

'Monday 21 of March 1831

This is a dark morning. I went down with my child to Mrs Upcher's school. They want me to pay 2s. 6d. per quarter, but I will not, for I don't think he shall stop there any great length of time . . .'

The events of the autumn of 1830 had shown that, for the oppressed Norfolk labourer, the path of arson and violence led only to imprisonment and transportation for the men involved and great suffering for their families. But there was another less open way in which they could get back at those in authority and improve their lot materially at the same time. Cheating the excise officers, 'riding officers' or 'boat men' as they were known locally, could prove both profitable and exciting. Indeed most of the inhabitants of the Norfolk coast seem to have been in a conspiracy to outwit the excise officers either by taking part in smuggling or by turning a blind eye when necessary.

At most times, Banville had no sympathy with law-breakers, but he does seem to have shared the prevailing complaisant attitude to smuggling which was, in fact, so widespread as scarcely to be thought of as crime. In February 1833 Banville records a pitched battle between the excise officers and the men of Norfolk.

'Friday 28 of February 1833

This night the smugglers got a cargo at a place of the name of Kelling Hard and the boat men shot at them and broke a man's leg of the name of Ward of Hempstead. They got him to Cley and he is there; the leg is cut off. They says that the Lieutenant Howes [the excise officer] shot at them without asking any questions, so that is the way that they do kill men when there is no need for it, but all Englishmen is forced to shoot men and always was forced to do it in all parts of the world wherever they put their foot as we see it.

Tuesday 4 of March 1833

I went off to Weybourne. I saw James and we walked down to Mr Nurse's, a publican there. We drank 2 pots of beer. At the same time the riding officer [the excise officer who first discovered the smugglers] came in. He told us the whole tale about how the smugglers caught him and handcuffed him, but the other [his fellow-officer] got off. By that means the alarm was made . . . They took one man [Pigle of Baconsthorpe] besides the poor man that lost his leg. The other man is to lie in prison for 12 months or pay £100, but it is not likely for him to get it paid, a poor man.'

> This was a more serious incident than might appear from Banville's account. According to the contemporary newspaper report, over a hundred men and more than twenty carts were involved, so that, even allowing for journalistic exaggeration, it was no small operation. Two excise officers on patrol at Kelling were warned of the presence of the smugglers by the barking of their dog. Half of the smugglers ran off immediately the alarm was raised, but between forty and fifty men stayed to fight it out with the coastguards. The first riding officer was captured at gun-point and handcuffed, but his companion escaped and ran to fetch help from the coastguard station. A pitched battle took place, the men using bludgeons and stones, and the smaller force of excise men and coastguards using pistols and cutlasses. Lieutenant Howes wounded several men and broke two pistols in the course of the fight, but only Ward, who lost his leg, and Pigle, were actually captured. The next morning a local fisherman found the beach littered with 'tubs and packages . . . of tobacco and brandy . . . upwards of 200 in number. The value of the whole is variously estimated from eight to twelve hundred pounds.'
>
> The incident was still in Banville's mind later that month.

'Friday 22 of March 1833

This morning James P. came to ask me to go to Kelling to shoot some grey plover with young Bolding and himself which I did . . . I seen the place where Ward was shot in the leg by the coastguards, the blood lies on the top of the field at present.'

Banville seems to have been reasonably happy at this time. By autumn 1833 the two younger Buxton boys, Thomas Fowell and Charles, were considered old enough to go out shooting with Larry ' just as Edward and Harry had done in earlier years.

'Wednesday 27 of November 1833

This day was a day of sport for me and my 2 young masters, T. F. Buxton and C. Buxton. I had all the rabbit holes well stopped down and ferreted, by that the rabbits was all out in the coverts there. 15 men and boys . . . all joined to help to show the young gents sport as they thought that they were worthy of it, and I must say they are nice young gentlemen at present. There was 25 dogs and happy was he that could make the most noise . . . I got 2s. 6d. worth of beer for the men . . .'

Larry enjoyed taking the boys out and gave up many hours of his spare time to skin birds for them. On one day he skinned eight birds, two woodpeckers, a gull, an owl and a fieldfare and three different divers. In May 1834 he proudly transcribed into his diary a letter written to him by Charles Buxton while the family was in London. He describes it as 'the first to me, a poor servant'.

'Dear Larry,

How are you and your wife and your children? I am very nicely after having the scarlet fever. Have you got any vipers or snakes and will you remind all the gamekeepers and woodcutters and rabbit-catchers and everybody who could catch us some vipers or snakes or slow worms.

Is there much game this year? How is Parsons and what do you think of Toll's pups? We have named them Mite and Minkin and Marls. What manner of greyhound is there which came for Fowell and me? Do you know what its name is? Is it a male or female? Is it black or white or what colour, is it old or young, small or large, ill or well? How is Dash and Maycock? Dash is not gone to Africa I suppose you know. Will you ask Parsons or anybody at Northrepps to look thoroughly through Roughton Heath for vipers please. If anybody catch any, let them catch them alive and put out their teeth and keep them in our snake box and provide them with water and fresh grass every day, or else hay which must be changed once a week, and water every other day, and 2 small frogs or lizards must always be with them. Now and then let them have a run in the grass, but watch exactly. Goodbye.

Your friend,
Charles Buxton'

Happy in his relations with the two young Buxtons, Larry was also delighted with the game figures for the 1833–4 season, since they showed the superiority of Sheringham over Weybourne in all kinds of game excepting wild-fowl and snipe. 1834 began with a splendid New Year dinner and a very profitable settlement day.

'Wednesday 1 of January 1834

This morning I got all things ready and drove my wife to Northrepps Hall where we were to dine, and the day was rather stormy, but still it turned out fine. There were all things that the heart of man could wish for dinner. 21 sat down to dinner besides the servants of the Hall. The evening passed off in all kinds of merry-making which was a great thing to see at a nobleman's house in Norfolk. We all after dinner went to see the fine spruce trees that fell with the storm, which was about 50 or perhaps 60 of them. It put me in mind of the time that I went to Stockholm to see it as there were thousands thrown up in all forests.

Tuesday 28 of January 1834

This morning I got a lend of my father-in-law's horse, drove off to Northrepps where I settled with pleasure with my worthy master who appeared in good humour . . . Here is what he done for me. He made [me] a present of £10 for keeping the rabbits down so well and £2 was above the expenses of them which he gave me and £5 for the use of my pony that the young gentlemen had to ride all the winter, that made me get £17 this day to help me on, which I think a deal of it.

Monday 31 of March 1834

. . . wrote to my father telling him what a blessing it was for his son to get to live with such a man in this country as T. F. Buxton Esq. MP . . .'

In the summer of 1833 Parliament finally passed the Act for the Abolition of Slavery within the British Empire, just a week after the death of the father of abolitionists, William Wilberforce. Priscilla

[133]

Buxton, now an able secretary to her father, wrote to a friend, 'Would that Mr Wilberforce had lived one fortnight longer, that my father might have taken back to him FULFILLED the task he gave him ten years ago'.

As Emancipation Day approached, great preparations were put in train. The main celebration was to be at Sheringham with Mrs Upcher as 'Mistress of the Fête'. The Buxtons were busy with their own preparations, for Friday, 1 August was also to be Priscilla Buxton's wedding day. She was to marry Andrew Johnston of Renny Hill, Fifeshire, Member of Parliament for St Andrew's. It was a marriage that the Buxtons fully approved, though her father bemoaned the loss of Priscilla's services, describing her as 'after Macaulay, my best human helper'.

Banville shared in the pride of the occasion, but he could not resist making some pointed comparisons between the condition of the slaves and that of the Norfolk labourers.

'Wednesday 30 of July 1834

I received a medal of Miss Buxton and my wife a silk handkerchief and a pair of gloves, all favours to remember the first of August. I saw Mrs Upcher this evening – she is highly pleased that this day is so fast coming, but here is my mind, that I would like to see a little more liberty for us here before we trouble about foreign parts.

Thursday 31 of July 1834

I went off to Bodham, then to Weybourne with James Parsons . . . to see if the bells would ring tomorrow, but there were no bell to ring there. James set off to Holt to strive to get popguns to fire them off, sport I do not like, but still for T. F. Buxton's honour I shall be happy to see all things got for the day . . . Now we shall all see if we live what this will do for us poor creatures as we are in the 3 kingdoms where there is no liberty for us . . .

Friday 1 of August 1834

This morning we got my breakfast at an early [hour], then my wife and I went to the Schoolroom to [hear] Mrs Upcher read for us all and then . . . Robert Long of Lower Sheringham to pray for us and to tell us all about the benefit it was to the slaves. It was a dark day in this part, but it was a bright one for the slaves . . . some say that they are better off than the men in this part . . . I then went and carved for breakfast and plenty of good meat were there also at dinner, but I did not taste of the meat. There were 30 at the table, all eat of it only myself. [As a Catholic Banville could not eat meat on a Friday.] After grace was over the health of Andrew Johnston Esq. and Mrs Johnston was drunk, and Mrs Upcher and the young ladies and the gentlemen, then Mr Buxton and all the family, all of course was crowned with the old token belonging to the Britons in all parts, 3 times 3 to all the party.'

The *Norwich Mercury* gives this account of the morning.

'The morning of this unrivalled, this glorious day, was ushered in by the chimes of the church bells – flags were seen flying and by half past seven o'clock Mrs Upcher and her family, with a number of the tenants, labourers, fishermen and children, were assembled in the village schoolhouse, where the joyful words met the eye "Slavery died today", inscribed on the wall, in letters tastefully formed of laurel leaves.'

Toasts were drunk to 'The Mistress of the Fête and her family', to 'King William and his 800,000 free subjects' and finally to 'Mr Buxton and the bride and bridegroom'. In the afternoon there were games and dancing and sports of all kinds including two cricket matches. Then more than a hundred and eighty children sat down to tea and were served with 'buckets of tea' and 'panniers of cake'. After sunset there was a bonfire. Banville takes up the story of the day –

'At about 9 o'clock there were a fire lit – it looked noble. I think at the least there were 300 or 400 children at this place at about 6 o'clock this evening. All kinds of amusement was there, they were all quite merry. I wish that they may have the grace of God in their hearts for ever more.

Mrs Upcher wore the medal against her heart and a small laurel brooch tied with white and black and I done the same, and a great many more had the laurel but not the medal of liberty.'

At Northrepps, meanwhile, there had been a great gathering of relations, friends and Abolitionists. Gifts of plate were presented to 'Buxton the Liberator', and Priscilla was duly married. 'Both spoke well', wrote Miss Buxton, 'and Mr Johnston's "I will" was *resolute*'. That afternoon Buxton sent a note down to Mrs Upcher –

'My dear friend, The bride is just off. Everything has passed off to admiration, and there is not a slave in the British colonies'.

There was a holiday atmosphere about that summer of 1834. Another family wedding took place in September, when Mary

Upcher, the eldest of Mrs Upcher's daughters, was married to the
Buxtons' cousin, Edmund.

'Wednesday 3 of September 1834
This day Mr Edmund Buxton was married to Miss Mary Upcher, the eldest
daughter of Mrs Upcher of Sheringham, a fine couple they were. I believe
they were true lovers if such was ever the case with the rich as I believe is
not often the case. There were a great many at church to see them married,
more than I ever saw before in the church . . . There were 3 pails of beer,
what was that to so many people as there were there? There [were] fire
rockets, they was fine ones. They had a fine fire there too which it looked
well and all other amusements such as turnipins . . . they set off to the cottage
at Northrepps . . .

Thursday 4 of September 1834
. . . I am sorry to say that at the Cottage last night, as they were firing off
the guns, one of them burst and killed William Curtis of Cromer, a blacksmith
by trade. What a dreadful thing for his wife and children. I forgot today that
there were good breakfast for us at Mrs Upcher's on the wedding day, but
no dinner but bread and cheese and the fragments of a wild turkey that they
had for their dinner . . .'

Long hot days, troubled only by a plague of 'mingeons' followed in
late September and early October. Then, on the day of a memorable
picnic at Beckham, the weather broke up in spectacular manner.
Thomas Fowell and Sam Hoare had been shooting during the
morning and the ladies joined them at Beckham church, then a
picturesque ruin.

'Anna Gurney, 1795–1857' by George Richmond. Despite suffering polio in early childhood,
she swam, shot, fished and travelled extensively. She was a considerable scholar and
could chat to shipwrecked sailors in several languages.

Sarah Maria Buxton, 1789–1839, T. F. Buxton's sister and companion to Anna Gurney,
with whom she founded the Belfry School at Overstrand. Portrait by George Richmond.

Overleaf: A great gale struck the Norfolk coast on Tuesday 16 February 1836 and lasted for
almost a week. John Berney Crome painted this picture of Yarmouth during the storms. Larry
describes several shipwrecks at Sheringham during the gales and the loss of the Billiard Room
at Cromer in a cliff fall.

'Tuesday 14 of October 1834

There they took lunch and the day was beautiful. Mr Hankinson, a parson of the new religion was with us, as fat as any other of the well-fed tribe. He folded his arms and gave us a few words about the dust of our forefathers . . . Then, and this I shall think of all the days of my life, the heavens darkened and the lightning and the claps of thunder came and torrents of wet, and so quick that we could not go one field to the farmhouse where Mrs Rounce lived and got the ladies in. They were forced to be undressed 3 of them and put into one bed. Mrs Hoare was out on a visit to a man of the name of Parson Robertson that . . . lived at Baconsthorpe. She came and T.F.B. took her in his arms and showed her the children, as he called them, then he rode home, sent his carriage for them and a change of raiment. 5 of the party went to bed at this house . . .'

> It was a good season for game of all kinds. In addition to the usual pheasants and partridges, Larry shot some snow bunting, Fowell and Charles each shot a wild turkey presumably strayed from Holkham, Arthur Upcher shot a deer escaped from Felbrigg and Mr Buxton succeeded in hitting even rarer game.

'Wednesday 12 of November 1834

T. F. Buxton Esq. M.P. shot me at the top of Weybourne Long Plantation with 1 grain in the chin which is very troublesome at this present time, 9 o'clock, but there is no one in the world have a better right to shoot Poor Larry than his honour.'

> Northrepps Cottage, at which the fatal accident had taken place during Edmund Buxton's wedding celebrations was very close to the Hall, and the 'Cottage Ladies', Sarah Buxton and Anna Gurney, always made the family welcome there.
>
> Charles Buxton, writing of the Cottage in his memorial of his father, says
>
> > 'The path to it from the Hall lies through the woods; and thither he [Mr Buxton] always turned his steps when his spirits needed

---

'The rescue of a crew at Gorleston, Norfolk' painted by John Cantiloe Joy, showing the use of Captain Manby's apparatus. The lifeline was fired to the ship from a gun on the beach, enabling people to be drawn ashore from the sinking craft.

Northrepps Cottage, built in 1793, was the home of the 'Cottage Ladies' after 1825. It was provided for Anna Gurney by her father and she died there in 1857.

to be enlivened, or his anxieties shared; well knowing that his presence would ever be hailed with eager delight'.

Banville never had anything but good to say of the Cottage Ladies. Their generosity was a by-word and their devotion to good works was total. They ran the Belfry School, supported both Bible and Missionary Societies and gave all the help they could to Buxton's work, taking on some of his paperwork after Priscilla's marriage. It was their special pleasure to give a good dinner to the beaters after one of the New Year shoots – 'the best beef and soup of the best' writes Banville, 'all the maids to wait on them. What a treat for poor men that hardly ever taste of the like'.

Neither lady enjoyed good health and Anna Gurney was, in fact, confined to an invalid carriage following a childhood attack of polio. Nonetheless Miss Gurney was a remarkable lady. She travelled widely and was a considerable scholar, publishing her own

Anna Gurney took a great interest in an improved version of Captain Manby's gun and in 1828 she organised a demonstration in the garden at Northrepps Cottage. In this drawing, made by Hannah Buxton, Anna is to be seen directing the local fishermen from her invalid carriage.

translation of the *Anglo-Saxon Chronicle*. She also took a very close and practical interest in the most up-to-date methods of preserving the lives of sailors caught in the treacherous storms and currents off the North Norfolk coast. As was seen in an earlier chapter, she gave early encouragement to the use of the mortar gun and in 1823 she had bought the improved version from Haze of Saxthorpe and presented it to the Mundesley life-boat.

The mortar gun was much in use during 1835 and 1836 – years of particularly fierce storms.

'Monday 26 of December 1835

I set off to Weybourne . . . There were a small vessel coming in to the shore, hundreds of all sorts running to see if they could render any assistance. The gun was there, but I am sorry to say that through mismanagement of the Lieutenant of Weybourne all the crew was lost in the watery grave. The sea was very rough and cold . . .

Wednesday 17 of February 1836
The day was a gale indeed, as the sea run mountains high along this coast, the wind almost to the north. The cliff at Cromer is hurting much and all of it was a gale.

Thursday 18 of February 1836
This day was the same as yesterday, 2 ships drove ashore at Cromer. I am sorry to say that 5 of the men was drowned and 1 man out of a billiard-room of Simey Simons of Cromer. It was built on the cliff. [The room and part of the cliff were washed away by the exceptionally high tide. The man had been attempting to rescue furniture and his body was later recovered at Bacton.] The poor man left a wife and 3 dear children to bewail his loss. Lord Suffield gave the widow £5; a good thing of his Lordship.
Just as the night was setting in a vessel came ashore at Sheringham. There were no great swell at the same time on the beach, but all was safe landed which was a good thing to see . . .
I can say there were hundreds of all sorts on the beach. Arthur Upcher gave a dinner to all of them that went out in the life-boat . . . a good thing of him to do it.
The Lieutenant of the Station here was in the boat, but the men threw him out of the boat which they had a just right to do as he is no friend to anyone in this part of the globe . . .

Friday 19 of February 1836
. . . The ship that came ashore yesterday it will become a wreck. There is one side of her burst and the coal all going out in the sea . . . It is low water and all the people is getting the coal as fast as they can with the boats.'

It seems certain that the Cottage Ladies retained the love and affection of the people of Northrepps and the surrounding area for their good works, for when Sarah Buxton died suddenly in August 1839 the attendance at her funeral was quite remarkable. It appears from a letter in the Gurney collection that Anna and Sarah had promised each other that, in the event of one of them dying away from home, the survivor would bring her home to be buried next to Harry Buxton in Overstrand Church. Sarah died while staying at Weymouth; Anna faithfully kept her promise and the funeral was held at Overstrand.

The pages of the diary covering the period are missing, so we have no words from Banville on this event, though he was almost certainly present. There survives, however, a loving description of the funeral written by Hannah Buxton.

'I cannot describe the luxuriance of beauty at the Cottage. The greenness was dazzling in the brilliant sun; the lawn gay with dahlias and scarlet geraniums, the fern-hill so gay and various . . . Between the pond and the Cottage stood a multitude, composed of her school children, boys and girls, the former in black pinafores, the latter in black frocks, and their teachers, and fishermen without number. At last the hearse appeared crossing the lawn from the garden door. We all fell in behind, the children etc. forming a line up each side, singing as we traversed that beautiful sloping field and up the lane. The Cromer people joined us on the way, her Bible Committee, and almost everyone else . . . Then we all went into the church, the coffin first, borne by twelve fishermen, full of grief; next was Cousin Anna in her chair. The tiny church was crowded, almost everybody in black; the old ruins, with the grand sea through the broken arches, and the perfect rest and quietness of the place, were striking. There was variety of feeling as we entered. The vault was open, and dearest Harry's coffin before our eyes. Cousin Anna sat at the head of the vault, between it and the church, Spinks and Stephen leaning on the back of her chair, looking as if their hearts would break, and all the maids behind them . . . Uncle Cunningham mounted a grave, and gave us a very striking address . . . he beautifully described her character, her spirituality, her hopefulness, her charity and close faithfulness to all around her.'

Chapter Ten

RETURN TO IRELAND
1836

Early in the New Year of 1836, Larry's thoughts were turning
further afield. His master had told him he might take a month off
to visit his family in Ireland. There is no indication in the diary as
to what prompted this trip at this particular time.

The week prior to his departure was one of keen anticipation of
the pleasures of seeing his father and all his old friends.

'Monday 22 of February 1836
T. F. Buxton, Esquire, M.P. was in the best of good humour all day. His
honour told me to start for Ireland next Thursday if all is well. He also told
me to buy a good horse or two if I could find them and money was no object
if they were first raters.

I am thinking of Ireland.'

Leaving his wife and children in Norfolk, Larry alone made the
journey and appears to have had a thoroughly enjoyable holiday.

'Thursday 25 of February 1836
This morning I set off to Wells [-next-the-Sea], a nice shipping village, not a
large one. I got something to eat myself and some also for the man that drove
me here. I ne'er was served as I was here – in the Tap a man was standing
and I said that I wanted a pencil which this man said that he would go and
get me two which I gave him one shilling. He came back with two penny
ones and as the coach was going away, he said they cost sixpence apiece.
What a theft in the broad day! I only mention this as a warning to all that
will travel through this county.

I now passed Holkham Hall. I saw Mr Coke, also her Ladyship, there
going out in the coach and here it put me in a stand to see that her Ladyship
was lying down by the side of her husband. I should think that she might
think it enough to lie at night by him.'

Thomas Coke had married Lady Anne Keppel, daughter of the
Earl of Albemarle in 1822. She was his second wife. He fathered
five children whilst in his seventies and family tradition has it that
it was a very happy marriage. When spotted by Larry Banville on
this occasion, he was in his eighty-second year and obviously still
very lively. The following year he was created 1st Earl of Leicester.

'I was in at Lynn by half past five o'clock. Went up to Mr Sharford. He told
me the best thing for me was to go to London by the coach that was to start
off at six o'clock or thereabouts. I set off with it. The night was fine. One of
the nastiest men was a guard that I ever saw. He keeped all alive up to
London. Friday the 26th at six o'clock was the hour we arrived in to London.
There were a coach there going in to Bristol which, of course, I set off with
it. A day of greater storm I ne'er was out in – wind, rain and snow was
coming right ahead of us the whole way. I passed a few poor horses that fell
in the road from hard driving. On my way I took some brandy to keep the
cold out.

At Bath at seven o'clock and then set off to Bristol at nine o'clock. At
Bristol got a fly. Went to where the packet is to sail from.'

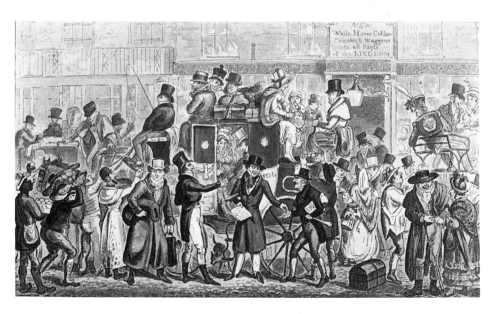

A cartoon by Cruikshank of the Bristol stagecoach about to set out from The White
Horse, Piccadilly. All the bustle of crowded coaches and busy preparations were
experienced by Larry on his journey to Bristol.

[143]

The following day the ship set sail in a storm. Larry was very sick
as was customary for him. He records that he paid two shillings
and sixpence for a sailor's berth.

'Sunday 28 of February 1836
Arrived at Ballyhack. Then Mr Goff and I got a horse and cart; went to the
pond at Haretown. There I saw two old maids. I think there is not a man in the
world would have anything to say to either of them for they are the picture of
dirt and filth, but, poor creatures, they were glad to see Poor Larry home again.

Now at home with my aged father and dear brothers. They all was happy
to see me.'

Now began a carefree holiday of mixed pleasures.

'I went to William Goff, Esquire. I saw Miss Lucy Goff, a fine lady. I often
was with her as children, though a servant. They were happy to see me.
They gave me some wine to drink.

Now I saw Miss Green that is now Mrs Hathen, a lady that I often had
on my knee when a child. I then set off to Mr Bird's and from that to C.
Henty's where he ordered Miss H. to give me a glass of punch. Then as I
was going out of the kitchen door I struck my eye against the door as it was
half open and dark. It made my eye become black.

Friday 4 of March 1836
This morning I set off to shoot across the country. I called at Andrew Dunn's
and also at Mr John Wilson's. I got a drop of whiskey at both places. Then
I came in at the Turnpence Gate. There I thought of my old master T. F.
Goff Esquire whom I thought a deal of and my tears came freely from me. I
wish I could shed tears of repentance for my poor soul. Then stopped the
evening with my friend John Cullen.

Sunday 6
This was a fine day. I set off to the chapel of Cullenstown where I heard the
Catholic clergy preach and saw a deal of people that I knew years ago. Then
we went into a public house to get a drop of beer, but nothing but whiskey
was to be had. My poor father drank a small share of it and was merry.'

Larry shot alone, with friends and even with the gentlemen who
were staying on the nearby estate of Tintern Abbey. He seems to
have enjoyed the reputation of being a good shot.

'Edward North Buxton' by George Richmond. Edward succeeded his father as second
baronet in 1845.

'A gentleman of the name of Mr Glasgow from New Ross came to shoot with us. It was to shoot against me that he came, but he was obliged to give in and start for home as I shot ten snipes, one partridge and a great tom cat in the bogs. Both gentlemen shot thirteen snipes between them both. I gave them the best of the shots as I did not fire at any birds that they could shoot at and a good many of mine I shot after they missed them. The snipes was wild and scarce in the quarter we shot this day, but it was all right for me to send the gent back again with news to Ross that the old keeper of T. F. Buxton, Esquire, M.P. showed him how snipes fell to an old gun not worth five pounds, as they styled it, but it cost forty guineas when new and it do well now if held right . . . I have seventy-seven snipe now. I am to send the whole to T. F. Buxton to London by the packet from Waterford. My brother Paddy is to go with them to Waterford in the morning.

Tuesday 15 of March 1836
I called to my Uncle Paddy's. I was at my father's by eleven o'clock and was surprised that the snipes did not go by the packet. The Captain would not allow them aboard as there were no one to take care of them at Bristol.

My uncle told me of a story. This he tells me happened a few weeks ago. A girl went and sold a pig for five or seven pounds and she was afraid that she would be robbed of it if she would go home late in the evening. The master of the house said if she liked to sleep with his daughter she might. As she, poor creature, was tired she went to bed and a young woman came in and said that she should sleep by the bed stack which, of course, she did, but could not close her eyes. When the girl came, she got in by the wall and fell asleep, but this girl could not sleep. At last she heard a good deal of chat in the kitchen and one of them said, "It is sharp enough". By that, she tied her packet about her and went and lay by the wall. They came into the room in the dark and cut their own child's throat and when they were all in a bustle, as anyone may expect they were, this girl slipped out as there were no notice of her taken at the time. Good fortune for her, two Cork men was on the road. They are the same as the carriager [carrier] in England. She cried to them that her life was in their hands and they covered her up in the cart as well as they could. Hardly had it done when the two that had killed the girl came up to them and asked them did they see a mad woman pass by. "Yes" was the answer, "for she must be mad for she passed by naked and she went

'Catherine Buxton, wife of Edward North Buxton, with her son Francis' by George Richmond.

as if she flew". They, of course, set off but they left the girl at the Police
Station and took the men. What a blessing for the poor creature!'

On the following evening the conversation continued in similar
vein –

'Mr Goff told me a queer story this night of two that was courting when
young . . . They were of great families. They lived in Waterford. First they
swore to each other that whichever would be called first would come and
appear to the living one. It happened to be the gentleman. He came to her
in the middle of the night and she was then in bed with her husband and he
was asleep at the time. He told her not to waken him and said that he would
die in six months and that she would be married again and that he would use
her very bad. Also she would die at the age of 39 years and to lead her life
as well as she could. She would not believe him that he was departed this
life so he put all the bed curtains through one of the rings and said, "Should
I touch you, the mark will follow you all your life." That, she said, she did
not care about, so he put his finger and thumb on her wrist and he told her
not to let anyone see it. Next morning she sewed a bit of black ribbon about

Hostility to the burden of tithes ran high in Ireland and occasionally erupted into violence.
This clash at Carrickshook in 1833 left eighteen policemen dead.

[146]

it and it remained so until her death. Her picture is to this day with the family with the ribbon around the wrist.'

> Other more serious matters were of equally absorbing interest. The collection of tithes was a burning issue in Ireland during these years. Most of the land was owned by Protestant absentee landlords; most of the tenants were Catholic. Tithes were levied on the tenant rather than on the landowner and so the situation existed where the Catholic tenant was compelled to pay a tenth of his income to the Protestant Church. Opposition in Ireland flared into violence during the early 1830s and Larry records that he attended one of the opposition meetings.

'Sunday 13 of March 1836

I went to the Chapel where there were at least three hundred men and a deal of others. Father Ryan preached for us. There were a paper to be signed. There were a great many that signed their names – I for one. They all do declare that they will not pay the tithe. I do not blame them a bit if they can get off it.'

> Unfortunately, Banville tells us very little of his family in Ireland. There are no descriptions of people or of the house and even his father and brothers are mentioned only in passing. He seems to have had a large number of relatives in the neighbourhood whom he visited.

'I stopped at Pat Barry's and my Uncle Matthew was chiefly singing for me. My uncle sang songs about O'Connell, but that is all well as he is opening men's eyes through the kingdom. Mr Barry wrote two songs for me to take to England . . .

I came to see my Aunt Poll that was married to an old man of the name of Hollison more for the sake of his money than for himself. I got a bit of dinner there . . .

My brother Paddy is married and his loins produced one son of the name of Martin called after our dear brother who is dead.

Tuesday 22 March 1836

I set off to shoot to Adamstown where I was to sleep the night and left my clothes with my brother John to take next day to the stone pond that I might dress and take the snipes that I would shoot the next day to Lord Carew of Castle Boro as I think it will show a little respect to his Lordship.

Wednesday 23 at Adamstown

This morning it was a storm of rain. It was so much that it put me rather out of temper. I was obliged to wait for my brother John until eleven o'clock as I had not powder or shot to start with and when he came so tired, the same as if he was after walking twenty or thirty miles, I gave him two glasses of the cursed thing of the country. The day was rather against my sport, but I shot pretty well. Now I am at the inn at the stone pond and to my great surprise no brother here as we can find. I, wet through and four or five miles to walk to the castle and it getting late and I have to walk back again to the inn where I started this morning. But at a short time my brother John made his appearance with a few of his half-naked friends and I was almost ashamed to own him as he was as drunk as any lord. I got half a pint of whiskey for himself and his friends to drink. I myself hated it although I took a drop of it to keep the cold out. I then dressed in a smoking room, then packed up my snipe. Set off to the castle. I sent the snipes in to his Lordship. Then he sent me five shillings to drink. I was much obliged to him. Then returned to the inn. There were my brother still drinking and as drunk as a beast and he wanted me to stop there all night. But I took my gun and my bag and told him to stop if he please. He then followed me. There were an open ford of water in the way – nothing only large stones about a yard apart that a man could get across dry – but his head was too light for his foot to keep on the stones and in he went. I was a good way before him, but I keep my ears open so as to hear him paddle in the water. By so doing he got through and it made him a little sober. What a shocking thing it is of a man to be so fond of the whiskey in this part.'

> Following his master's instructions, Larry tried to obtain some good horses at Taghmon fair, but without success. He continued to keep his eyes open, but found nothing that 'would suit T. F. Buxton'.

'I shot across the country to Mr Andy Neil's to see a horse he had, but it was nothing but legs.'

> As March drew to its close, Larry's thoughts began to turn to his departure. He visited many friends to take his farewells and remarked sadly that he thought there were several whom he would never see again. He was particularly sorry to be leaving his father.

'My aged father when he heard that I was going away, he spoke no more. My heart was full to see it. My three brothers came to this place which I wished them goodbye. I left them bathed in tears as my dear brother Robin and father at home, I suppose for the last at this side of the grave . . . My brother Paddy came. We had a pot of beer for the last at this visit. I am to leave £2 with Mr Goff for him as I think that it will be a little help for them as my father is still alive and very feeble in person.'

On 29 March, Larry arrived in Waterford to board the steamer. It sailed the following morning.

'The wind rose a fine breeze. When we were taking our farewell of the lighthouse, the sea run mountains high. I shortly got sick as usual. I never was in a vessel at sea that creaked so much and then to add to the noise were 700 or perhaps 750 pigs aboard that joined in the music for they were, one or another, squealing the whole way. In safety at Bristol about four o'clock. Set off for London . . . I may say I have paid the last visit to my mother country.

London – 1 April 1836
The coach left the mail in Piccadilly and then drove to Lady Lane and there I dressed in the stable . . . I set off to Devonshire Street [the Buxton's London house] where I saw all the servants. They all was happy to see me back again. I also saw T. F. Buxton who told me that he was off for Weymouth in the morning. I wished him a good journey and a safe return to Norfolk.

I wrote a note to my wife to say I was in London. T.F.B. was so kind as to frank it to his son, Edward, at Cromer with orders to send it to my wife as soon as he would get it. I must say it was very kind of this noble man to do for me.'

The following day, Larry visited the Buxton brewery and was shown round. He also visited the zoo.

'We went to the gardens where I saw the beaver, the only animal that I wished to see in it. But still there were all sorts there to see. I thought it very odd to see so many of the beauties of England stop against the monkeys as some of them were in their season. I asked one of the men – was it a usual thing for the ladies of London always to stop there? He assured me as follows. If there were three hundred of them to come in one day, two hundred and ninety-nine would fain stop there to view the tricks of the monkeys and they are said to be the dirtiest brutes in the gardens. What must a man think of them when they will go and sit down and feast their eyes with such things! I know that some of them are as full of lust as them they gaze on.'

[149]

Returning home from Ireland through London, Larry visited the Zoo in Regent's Park.

    After tea with the servants at the Buxtons' London house, he took
the coach to Norfolk.

'I put a Guernsey waistcoat on to keep me warm all night. The night was
stormy until we came to Newmarket. After that it was a heavy fall of snow,
but I did not feel cold as I was warm and well clothed with plenty of clothes.

    Five shillings it cost me to Cromer. I called at Northrepps. I there saw
my two masters and Richard Hoare and they seemed glad to see Poor Larry
again. I took the pony and rode off from Cromer. On my way I met Mrs
Alsop with my boy, Samuel. He was glad to see me. We returned to pay my
fare at Cromer. He had a gig and a horse there waiting for me. I met my
wife, four children and her sister, Catherine Lown, just at the mill. All was
happy to see me and I was the same as they were.

    Now I shall tell my reader the expense of my visit to see my native country,
but still I do not regret it, by no means, as it will be most likely the last time
in my life. My costs is £15. 10. 0. T. F. Buxton, Esquire, M.P. was so kind
as to give me £10 to help me over which was very kind of him to do. May
God reward him in due time for it.'

PART III

THE PASSING YEARS
1835–1869

Chapter Eleven

TROUBLE

1835–37

About a year before he went to Ireland, Banville had been placed in a serious dilemma. T. F. Buxton had gone to Weymouth to defend his Parliamentary seat, despite the family's worries about his health. He returned in January.

'Saturday 17 of January 1835
This morning they drove to my house in what I call flying style. The bridles was trimmed with blue ribbons [Whig colour at that time]. T. F. Buxton M.P. dressed at my house and they shot the dales . . . T. F. Buxton M.P. told me this day that Mr. Upcher would take the manor himself this season. What a change it is for us all, but I trust it will not make any great change for me. James Parsons said to me that he would ask T. F. Buxton to let me stop with him which was very kind of him, but I shall hear all about it in a few days . . .

Monday 19 of January 1835
. . . I was thinking a thousand times of what was going to be done with me in this part of the world. T. F. Buxton called me to him at different times the same as if he wanted to speak to me, but something came in the way . . .

Wednesday 21 of January 1835
. . . My master told me that Mr Upcher would take me with the manor if I liked, but if I did not like it and stopped with them, he should put me to the mill for this season and perhaps there might something else turn up in another year, but still his honour should give me my choice of the 2 places, but this is my mind, to stop with my 2 masters while they will keep me. At the close of the day T. F. Buxton called me to him and told Edmund Buxton to walk on [as] he had something to tell me. It was as follows, that I should tell him in the morning whether I would stop with them or not. At this moment I was so full that I hardly could speak a word, but this I said, if I left my 2 worthy masters whom I had the honour of serving for all [these] years and complied

[153]

[sic] to deprive them of their sport . . . and see them out shooting and not allowed to go to them, it would be more than I would be able to bear . . . At that moment S. Hoare Esq. took notice of what we were talking of and said . . . "It is rather hard on Larry to give his mind so soon. Go home, tell your wife, and she will give you good advice and what she will tell you, do it. You are at least 14 days our servant on the manor." Oh what passed into my spirits I cannot tell at that moment, for I believe . . . that any part of the kingdom would be more agreeable to me than where I would see my master out shooting at both sides of me.

I then came home in poor spirits, almost ready to burst into tears, waiting for the morning, but my mind is to stop [with] the old masters as long as they will keep me.

Thursday 22 of January 1835
This morning I set out to Mrs Upcher's where my two masters was at breakfast. The moment that T.F.B. was done his he called, "Larry" and said "How is it to be?" I answered, stop with his honour if he was satisfied with me. He smiled and said "It is all right." I again stood his servant.'

> The situation, however, was not satisfactory. Banville had no manor of his own, while the largest and best stocked manor, Weybourne, was left under the care of his rival, James Parsons.
> To make matters worse Buxton's health, strained by years of overwork, was deteriorating. Having already suffered a slight stroke in 1827 his friends were worried about his undertaking another Parliamentary session. Banville certainly began to find him changed.

'Thursday 30 of September 1835
. . . Now I must say that in all the days that I ever was out with the gentlemen in my life, I ne'er saw T. F. Buxton so much out of temper . . . everything was wrong, dogs was not right, wadding was not right, the powder horn was out of order [though] it was as usual, but we, both poor and rich, is sometimes out of our place.'

> On another day Larry noted that James Parsons, too, seemed out of sorts.

'Friday 29 of October 1835
James Parsons was not in the best of humour all day. I hardly knew what was the matter with him until the day's sport was over and to my great surprise he told me that the Dacks [presumably a local family] sent him a

writ from the Queen's [sic] Bench in London. It was for beating them on Sunday . . .

Ed. N. Buxton told him he ought to give them a good whipping, but the law will not allow any man to do so. By so doing he will be made pay for it where he might have made them pay as he found a trap in their pocket and they had no right to be there with it, but I must say James is rather fond of knocking men about, but it will not do in all cases.'

> One cold stormy Sunday in 1835, while his wife was at church, Larry sat down to write into the back of the second volume of his diary all the game figures he had collected over the years. At the end he wrote –

'This may amuse someone or other in the course of some future time when I am gone out of this part of the world, at least out of this blasted place of Sheringham, I believe one of the damnedest places in the kingdom.'

> Whatever his disappointments, Larry had obviously recovered his spirits in time for Christmas and for the New Year dinner at Northrepps.

'Friday 1 of January 1836
43 of us sat down to dinner at the Hall this day of all sorts that a man's heart could wish for. Out of all those they all eat of meat only myself. There were a fine piece of codfish for my dinner. There were plenty of puddings, also plain melted butter . . . plenty of wine and water for the females. We broke up at 1 o'clock and the frost was as hard as it was for many a day. We all gave the old custom of the Hall that was to cheer for the family in good English style, but eating and drinking is the only thing that they think of in this part of Norfolk.'

> On his return from Ireland in April Banville was given Beeston Manor to look after and quickly resumed his normal seasonal activities.

'Monday 25 April 1836
This was a fine day. I was at home the most of it as I wanted to boil my copper. I also worked in the garden. The day was so fine that I worked without my coat. I set a turkey with sixteen eggs. I sowed some potatoes, some radish seeds and turnip seed. I caught seven mice in traps since I

returned from Ireland and I caught two great old rats. There is a deal of people coming home from Holt fair, some of them drunk enough. When I was at the fair at Taghmon, I don't think I saw one drunk in it. What a blessing!'

> Larry's memory was rather short. Only a month before, after his visit to Taghmon fair, he complained of the whiskey drinking and wrote that 'I saw the men drinking it as if it was water'.

'Saturday 30 April

This morning I set off to Weybourne. James and myself went off to get some plovers' eggs as usual, but only got eleven of them that were good. At night I was not well. My dear wife said to me it was all fancy, that I need not be that way if I liked, but my spirits was low.

May, the first of the month, 1836

This morning the first thing that I saw was a boy of the name of Wagg stoning my turkeys in the road. The parson saw him also stealing the turkeys' eggs, but what could I do with a boy? . . . I have fifteen turkeys out. They are nice ones.'

> At this time Larry was very interested in the proposals to improve and extend the duck decoy near the Hall.

'Tuesday 10 May

This day was fine. I went into my garden a while, then took out two dogs for a while. Then after dinner I took my gun in my hand. Set off to Weybourne to speak to James Parsons, but he was out. I then saw Mr Philip Grice, the best net-maker in Norfolk. Told me all about the net for the decoy which it is as follows. The big end – near the pond, of course – comes first. This net is to be 28 yards long and 66 meshes of 4 inches each mesh and at each side of it . . . to be braided with 3 inch mesh. This is to be brought at the other end to 60 meshes. The second net is 4 inch mesh each with 50 [meshes] and the third net to be 50 yards long of 3 inch mesh and at the end of the 50 meshes to be brought to 3 or 4 foot in breadth. This will cover a fair size pipe for to take ducks in . . .

I met James on my way home and he told me that he was at Lord Orford's as he wanted to let his manor [of Weybourne]. James was very ill last Friday night as he tells me, but he is well at present.

I shot three rabbits this day. They were does.

Thursday 12 of the month

This day Mr Robert Sunman [a builder of Sheringham] and I went to see the decoy for taking ducks at Hempstead. He is a man that can sketch the buildings of any sort. He drew it for me . . .

Mr Sunman drove his pony and went to Wiveton Bell [public house] from that to Cley, from that to Weybourne. It is awful to see the walls and dykes along the village of Cley and Salthouse. They were broke down by the high tide . . . The water ran in to some of the houses four and five feet in depth. The old men or women ne'er saw such a high tide.

Monday 23 May 1836

This was a fine day. I went down to Mr Sunman's and he drew the draft of the duck decoy.

I then spent four pence for a pot of beer. Then, as it is a custom in Sheringham for us all to go to spend the evening at this season of the year with my father-in-law, we did – wife and children and all of his sons and all his son-in-laws like myself. Now I shall state what I saw and heard there this evening.'

> Here part of the page has been cut away as in other places in the diary where a piece of scandal or a family upset has been included. When the entry is continued, there is a hint that a quarrel took place between one of Sarah's brothers and old Mr Lown for Larry is in the middle of writing 'but he ought to [have] thought of the Scripture as it is written "Honour thy father and mother" . . . May God give him grace to think of it and to beg his earthly father's forgiveness'. Larry was certainly shocked by the episode, concluding

'We left it at 10 o'clock quite disgusted at what we heard there this evening.'

> The summer saw Larry tying fishing flies for the Buxton boys to take on their forthcoming holiday. Mr Buxton had decided to take the whole family up to the grouse moors for the summer and by July Larry was busy with his own preparations to leave Norfolk for he was to join them in Scotland.

'Friday 16 July

This day I got a horse of my father-in-law's. Set off to the Hall to see if any of the shooting clothes would do for the moors as T. F. Buxton is thinking of going there. I brought two coats, two pairs of shoes, three pairs of gaiters, one pantaloons. I bought silks of all sorts in Cromer to tie some flies so that I shall have some of all colours of my own. My son Samuel went with me.

[157]

Tuesday 19

I went to Mr Dagless of Bodham. He is a blacksmith. I got a hoop made for a landing net and sent it to Weybourne to get a net put to it.

Wednesday 20

I tied 17 flies. I shot 2 larks as I wanted their wings for the flies as I have to tie different sorts.'

> During his absence, Buxton seems to have entrusted some of his
> affairs to Mr Johnson, a local lawyer. Banville clearly did not like
> the man and some of his complaints about him are still in the diary,
> though others have been cut out.

'Johnson, a lawyer of Runton, got all our accounts or, at least, the money of them. This summer half-year – James for Weybourne £51. 11. 0., Larry £67. 6. 11., Payne £20. 0. 0., Platten £26. 2. 2. which was a deal of money. Now a little was sent in care of him for me, £20 in it for me to take me to the north. This fine gentleman took the liberty of opening my letter and was going to give that money to Payne. I do not understand that a learned gent would do such a thing as to open a letter not of his own, but a poor man can do nothing in this country or any place else.'

> At the beginning of August 1836, Larry and his dogs set off for
> Scotland, sailing up the east coast to Newcastle and then travelling
> on by coach. It was a trying journey with missed boats, drunken
> sailors, gale-force winds, Larry and his dogs lying in a heap, all
> being sick together and ending with resentment about a disagree-
> able coachman. A week later they all arrived in Edinburgh. Larry
> was impressed with the city.

'This was a fine day. I walked about as I was here by myself. I went up to where Lord Nelson's monument is as a man can nearly see all over the old city as well as the new town. It was a beautiful sight for me to see . . . This hill that I am speaking of it is called Calton Hill where the Jews are buried in a large vault or cave as they are not allowed to be interred in the churches. I saw King Arthur's Seat about a mile to the east of the city. It is a fine steep hill. The top of it appears mostly of rocks.'

> Larry waited at an Edinburgh inn for instructions to arrive from
> his master. He reflected that –

'I am just the same as if I fell into a new world. I know no one in this great city, but if I was a young man and wanted a wife and could maintain one in any part where I please, this is where I should come to find one.'

Finally, orders reached him to go to Perthshire. He took a fly-boat – a fast, flat-bottomed craft – and sailed along the Union and Clyde Canals to Glasgow. He found the journey particularly interesting.

'I passed one of the king's palaces and also the greatest ironworks in the three kingdoms. The crops of all sorts looks well on both sides of this water . . . We went a third of a mile through a tunnel. This was a frightful thing to see it going underground.'

At Glasgow he took the steamer to Dunbarton, then a coach to the south end of Loch Lomond, a steamer to the north of the Loch and a horse and cart to Tyndrum. Finally, two days later he reached Dalmally.

'Now, about 8 o'clock at Dalmally, a forlorn looking spot. The appearance of them that keep the inn is, I fear, very bad. I am here also in the middle of strangers and I must say that I like all those wild parts rather well.'

The Buxtons' host for the shooting season was the Marquis of Breadalbane, a regular attender of the House of Lords and a London friend of Buxton.

Three days later, Larry received a letter from Buxton to say that he would be arriving shortly. Larry unpacked all the shooting things ready for his master's arrival.

'Tuesday 16 August 1836

This day I shall say nothing of until 10 o'clock at night when I heard that T. F. Buxton and all the party was near at hand. The most of them shook me by the hand. Fifteen of them came – I made the sixteenth of the train. What a lot to find food for in this part of the Highlands.'

The following day the shooting and fishing got under way.

'This day I was out on the moors with the guide and T. F. Buxton, Mr Johnston, both Members of Parliament. The day was wet, the whole of it. It was a sorry day's sport as the reader will see . . . I hunted the dogs, but I was sorry to see that T. F. Buxton was not fit for this country at this time of life as he was afraid to go on the side of the hills where he could be most likely to get shots. This man that was sent with us, he was as big a goose as

I ever saw out with a gentleman sporting, unless the man in the Orkneys that stop in the rain to keep the umbrella dry. I was sorry to see that the Honourable Member got a fall, but it was not of any harm.'

Day after day the sport was poor. The entry for 22 August is a typical one.

'This day was a day of wet. We went to the moors. T. F. Buxton wet through, also Larry and all the game was 1 grouse, 3 snipes, 2 blackgame. What a state to be in on the mountain – the dogs not worth a penny, the game scarce and the mountains half covered with snow, the valleys over flooded with the top rains from the hills.'

Larry joined the trip made by the family party to the Highland Games at St Fillan's.

'First the pipes all played. They were all dressed in the Highland dress, each of them in the tartan belonging to their own clan. They also danced, but I suppose they thought it grand, but I thought nothing of it. They fenced with sticks, but it was but a sorry one. Then the best men threw a sledge hammer

The running race at a Highland Games. 'They were all dressed in the Highland dress, each of them in the tartan belonging to their own clan . . .'

of the weight of 22 pounds 60 feet 4 inches. There were a ball of stone 22 pounds. They threw it 32 feet 4 inches. This was thrown by a man of Scotch parents, but brought up in England as they call him Scotch John there. There were a green larch pole of 17 feet long to throw it, but it should turn over which was hard work. The day passed off well in regard of sport. They finished the sport with firing, but that I did not go to set my eye on who would shoot the best.

I thought it hard to see my master a stranger there and no notice of him taken, but there were a tent for the shelter of the great ones, but not one of them took notice of Mrs and Miss Buxton. I asked the pony man that came with us as he was their own countryman if it was free for all to go into the tents. If so, I should like to see my two ladies in it. He went off for a while, but came back and said he saw no one that he could ask. I walked to Mrs Buxton and gave her my big coat to sit on also to stand on it as the ground was very damp as there were such a fall of rain in the morning.'

> The family moved on to Renny Hill, the home of Priscilla and her husband Andrew Johnston . . . Little shooting was done, however, as Buxton was ill. When he recovered, the party travelled to Taymouth Castle, the seat of Lord Breadalbane. The entertainment was lavish, as Buxton described in a letter to Priscilla –
>
>> 'When I drove up in my Hack chaise, my arrival, like a knight of old, was announced by a blast on the Bugle . . . A harper played at one time under the window, then a band of five performers in the next room and the dinner was grandeur itself – fish from the lake, grouse and mutton from the hills, venison from the forest . . .
>>
>> The next morning after breakfast at which the Piper played – I mounted an excited pony, rode in fair weather up the mountain, saw the lake, the grounds, the hills in perfection.'
>
> Both Larry and his master admired Lady Breadalbane. Buxton thought her 'a charming creature' and Larry wrote

'I saw Lady Breadalbane. She is a fine looking lady. His Lordship is gone to shoot about thirteen miles from this place. They say his Lordship will not return until Monday. I should wonder, if it was my case, to let her Ladyship be there and I in another place. No, I should go and wander all the mountains in the day, but her I would be alongside of at night.'

[161]

It was here that Larry first met James Guthrie, the head keeper, with whom he kept up a correspondence for many years. Larry was invited to visit his house and see his collection of birds' and animals' skins.

'His house where he lives is a round tower. He have a deal of hawks' skins and wild cats' skins and a deal of ravens, all of which he trapped on the hills.'

After a stay of only a few days, Buxton decided to go to Edinburgh and Larry took the steamer south. The weather was too rough to land him on the Norfolk coast and he was forced to sail on to London. As usual, it was an unpleasant journey. The dogs were ill and two of them died at the end of the voyage. Finding that his master had not yet returned to London, he did not linger, but took the coach back to Norfolk.

'Saturday 24th
In Holt about half past 10 o'clock. The night fine. I walked home to Sheringham Lodge where I often wished to be since I left that part.'

Larry was not very happy during the months that followed his return from Scotland, and perhaps because of this he was sensitive to the plight of others and sceptical of some people's efforts to do good.
    After his successful campaign against slavery, Buxton turned his attention to a scheme to take the benefits of agriculture, commerce and a Christian education to the black people of West Africa. This plan was fully supported at Sheringham and Northrepps by frequent missionary meetings and sermons. Banville had his own view of such meetings.

'Sunday 2 of October 1836
This morning I went to church, then to Sheringham Hall in the evening to a missionary meeting and it was, I am happy to say, well attended, but it is all well for those gentlemen in this part to strive to make them believe that all others is in the dark and what a blessing it is for them to be in the light of the gospel. I could make some remarks on his speech, but I shall pass it by for the present . . . This kind of meeting is a nice thing for the girls and boys as they go there for no other purpose [than to meet each other] as I saw it this night while this fat-faced man was speaking to them all.'

Larry's visit to the workhouse at Sheringham a few days later must have made him wonder just how far the 'light of the gospel' really shone in Norfolk.

'Wednesday 5 of October 1836

I went down into town to see if I could have the pony to go to Northrepps. I paid Mr B. Chamberlain 2s. 1d for poor rates and spent 1s. 2d, then I went into the workhouse to see it.

What a disgraceful system is used there by the clergyman that is to preach for the poor. There is 2 rooms, or otherwise one large one and boards put in the middle of it. The parson is to stand so as to see into the 2 apartments, then the poor men is to be in one part, the women in the other and not to see each other . . . although been joined together by the same creed that they are under at this time. What a bottle of smoke and the cork out!'

The Poor Law of 1834 had stipulated separate workhouses for men and women, but many country districts could not afford new buildings and compromised by separating the groups within the same workhouse. The cruel separation of married couples under

The workhouse: husband and wife are separated.

[163]

this system caused trouble in many workhouses at this time and Banville noted in his diary a little later –

'At Gimingham the other night the men got each of them to their own wives and there is a great row about it. What a cursed law to take a man's wife away from them on account of being poor in this blessed country . . .'

This particular incident was not recorded in the newspapers of the day, but others were, including a deliberate fire at Rollesby workhouse resulting from anger over the separation of husbands and wives. When such incidents occurred it was not uncommon for inmates of workhouses to be committed to prison for three weeks for 'disorderly behaviour'.

Through that autumn Larry's resentment against James Parsons continued, for although Banville was the senior of the two it was James who was keeper of Weybourne, the best shooting ground on the estate.

'Wednesday 9 November 1836

I set off to meet the gentlemen and I had to carry three guns with me, but when I met James Parsons and boy they forgot T. F. Buxton's pouch – sent the boy back for it.

James told the gentlemen that the Hills was not ready to shoot and that there were nothing ready, but T.F.B. told him he had orders long enough before and shoot they would. What a thing for a keeper to tell his master! Now this same keeper was always bragging what a lot of game he and his covert had, but this was always the case with him since I saw him. He had nothing there, no powder and wadding, in a word nothing in the style of a keeper.'

Later in the month Banville's grudges gave way to grief through a local tragedy.

'Tuesday 29 of November 1836

. . . This evening as my son Samuel came from school he brought the doleful news that there were 7 men drowned at Lower Sheringham. It is the greatest number that they lost out of Sheringham for many a year. My heart was quite cold at the time I heard of it. They had no warning, the storm came so quick on them there were no time to run from it. It tore up a deal of trees on Sheringham estate, but I care not a farthing about them as they are but little value.'

[164]

The *Norfolk Chronicle* for 3 December 1836 refers to this storm as 'the most dreadful and sudden hurricane from the north-west ever remembered here'. Two Sheringham fishing boats were lost containing seven men and boys. Only one body was recovered and not a vestige of the boats. Those who died were William Little aged seventy-five, James, Paul and Robert Bishop aged twenty-two, sixteen and fourteen, John Wilson aged twenty-three and Cutler Crask and his thirteen-year-old son. Crask left a wife and seven children.

Early in the New Year Banville's general discontent with his situation and his increasing jealousy of James Parsons, combined with Mr Buxton's deteriorating health and judgement, brought about the first serious breach in the hitherto excellent relations between Larry and his master.

'Tuesday 17 January 1837

At this time T. F. Buxton is not in the best of humour with me. The reason is that I have not a first rate dog to pick up the birds. But if masters will not get them, where is servants to buy them? And I am at all calls while other keepers is sporting for their pleasure.'

Llewellyn Lloyd was visiting Norfolk at this time and his treatment by the Buxtons and the Upchers did nothing to improve Larry's feelings towards his master.

'This morning I went down to Mrs Upcher's where I see them set off to fox hunt and L. Lloyd and Howes and myself set off to Northrepps Hall. This was a trial to me to see that no grand cart was sent either for or with the stranger of as good blood as any in this kingdom, only the cursed gold not in his pocket. If it was, a carriage would be at the post for him. This shows what people is in this sinful world.

At night I went to see the wild beasts that was at Cromer, well worth to see. First I saw a horned horse that killed its keeper in 1831, a dreadful creature it is. The lions was beautiful to see, the tigers also was fine animals. Two of them were black. I saw a pelican, 70 years of age. It was white as a swan. I saw all in the show, paid 1s. for it.

I walked down this evening with L. Lloyd Esq. in to Cromer. This will tell the reader what it is to be without money at command. It was about 12 o'clock at night when Poor Larry went to his bed and a sorry one it was. I was in a state that I could not tell to my simple paper to see such things done to L. Lloyd, but this I must say that he ne'er murmured to me. If I was in his stead, I should think and say that when they should see my face again they would treat me like a gentleman.

'Thursday 26 of January 1837

This morning I wrote a note to James Parsons to let him know that he was to meet T. F. Buxton at Beeston or at Weybourne as he was to shoot by himself, but he came to Mrs Upcher's and stopped there until 11 o'clock. Then when the gentlemen came, he told my master that he could not shoot at the Hills at which my master was very angry with me, but took no notice of James . . . but he is not well at present and I always saw him willing to throw the blame on anyone before he would take it himself. I don't know what he would think of me if I should tell T. F. Buxton all I know about his doings, but it will overtake him when he least think of it.

They all dined at Mrs Upcher's and we got a bottle of wine for us and very good it was. I was obliged to speak to T. F. Buxton in the dining room and there he gave me a glass of wine, the first for this three months, but he want me to get good dogs, but if they were good today they would be bad on another. What he mean by treating me in such a manner as he do at present I am not aware of, but I should think that he would let it all out at the settling day.

Friday 3 of February

I fired powder over York and Bill until they pretty well dropped to the gun. Then set off to Beeston. I fired at a snipe – missed it. I shot two partridges with one shot.

I wrote the most of my bills this night as we must have a settling day in the course of a few days . . . At night it was cold and my spirits bad and my mind in the worst that I hardly ever was in such a state, and if death would come in a fair way it should be welcome to the poor Irishman in Norfolk, but still let the God of my fathers work His will.

Monday 6 February 1837

This morning I set off in such poor spirits that I ne'er went to settle with a gentleman before in my life. I set off at an early hour thinking to settle and have it over, but this was not the case as T. F. Buxton went out . . .

All dined in the servants' hall – plenty of roast beef and boiled beef and plum puddings, but still all this was not to cheer my spirits up.

Now comes the settling of my accounts. Powder and shot with wadding and repairs of guns was £20. 19. 6., game food £14. 2. 0., dogs' food for 8 months for 6 dogs was £7. 0. 5., for that time my wages was £31. 9. 7½. This made up in different shapes – a man for 8 weeks was £4. 16. 0., rent £5. 0. 0., poor rates 9s. 7½., sundries was £5. 19. 7., then watching £2. 8. 10d. He gave me a draft on the bank in London on Lloyd and Co.

Now the reader can see that there were no fault found with my accounts, and he said that he had nothing to say against my accounts, but here it comes. It is as follows as nearly as I can set it down. Three things. The first was that I told him in Scotland that a setter bitch had puppies and she had not. "No, sir, I told you that she had run to a dog when I was going and that I did not take her on that account."

The second was that I told him that we shot partridges at one side of the ground and that we shot at the other part. As for this charge when he asked me where did I shoot, I said that most of the birds was bagged on Mr Nurse's land, but did not say any more about it as I thought it not worth while.

The third was that I said that I seeked for a wounded partridge and I did not. "Yes, sir, I searched for it as far as I thought it useful, but I did not get it".

Now I spoke as follows, "Sir, I am under all sort of duty to you for the favours that I have received. Further I can say I should be very sorry to disoblige a master that behaved so kind to me and family since I came to be a servant, and this I can say, the next fault that is laid to myself, I freely give you leave to turn me away and let me get a new master some other place".

What three charges to bring against me after twelve years servitude . . . but this I must say he is a good master, but still all is not right in many respects.

Saturday 11 of February

. . . He is to start off for town on Monday next if all is well. I had but little chat with him, but the less the better.'

Chapter Twelve

THE CAPERCAILLIES

1837

In return for the hospitality shown him the previous summer by Lord Breadalbane, Buxton proposed in the early spring of 1837 to send Larry to Sweden to procure capercaillies for the Breadalbane estate at Taymouth. These great game birds, once indigenous to the British Isles, became extinct in England about 1660 and in Scotland in the 1770s, but were still abundant in Scandinavia. An unsuccessful attempt had been made to introduce a pair of capercaillies to the estate of the Duke of Fife in 1828 and another pair brought over the following year failed to produce surviving young. Buxton had been given two birds by Llewellyn Lloyd in 1825. From this pair, six young ones were hatched, but as a result of being in the hot sun for too long, they died and so did the hen. The cock was then released into the Cromer woods, but was accidentally shot two years afterwards.

A determined and carefully planned effort was now to be made. It was arranged that Larry should rejoin Llewellyn Lloyd in Sweden and that the two of them should collect the capercaillies together and organize their transport to Scotland.

The enterprise was first mentioned in the diary in August 1836 when Buxton spoke to Larry about the project. The following month he discussed the matter further with Larry and Lord Breadalbane's keeper, James Guthrie, when they were all out shooting together.

'T. F. Buxton, Esquire, told the keeper that he had wrote to a friend of his to get twenty of the great capercaillies for to stock this noble manor. The keeper told his honour that his Lordship was very fond of all kinds of wild beasts. I told the keeper that they were the finest birds in the woods. I saw three of them that was shot in Sweden – one old one and two young ones. The weight of them was 28½ pounds which put him to a stand to think what kind of bird they were.'

So, in the early spring, Larry began to prepare for his departure for Sweden. He sowed seeds in his garden, bought a hat and coat, equipped himself with fish hooks and visited many friends and acquaintances in the neighbourhood to take his farewells. By the end of March, relations between Larry and Mr Buxton had so far deteriorated that Larry wrote on the eve of his departure for Sweden –

'Mrs Upcher tells me that Sweden is about 550 miles across the sea. I wish I had not to be drove about like a slave as I am this last two years, for such a change ne'er took in a gentleman as there did in T. F. Buxton . . . I can wish with all my heart the journey was for thousands of miles and also for years to come. I should be glad of it although I am sorry to part with my home. But some thinks it is almost transporting me, but they are not aware of my mind at this present time as I must think that I am a burden to my master or at least he thinks so.'

He set off on Friday 30 March 1837. In contrast with his previous trip to Sweden, the account of this visit is full of details of all his expenses. It appears that he was expected to find the money for the journey and the cost of his keep and this was later refunded to him on his return. Larry received the highest wages amongst the keepers and this, together with the occasional tips from visiting sportsmen, obviously allowed for some savings to be made. In consequence, this arrangement for his travelling expenses was not too burdensome for him.

'This day I set off to Cromer and my eldest son with me. There I set off to Norwich. What it cost is: fishing tackle – six shillings, my coach fare was four shillings, porter – 6d, bed – one shilling.

Saturday 1 April
This morning I got up at an early hour. I bought a hat – 6/6d. My dog cost nine shillings to Ipswich. Here I shall stop all night at the sign of the Bull's Head. I took a walk through this town. It is, I believe, in a bad state. They are all cursing the Poor Law Bill. Perhaps it is all for the better, but the children and women looked most miserable.

Sunday 2 April
This morning I set off to the boat house where I was to go from, to Harwich, about eight miles down the river. I got aboard of the boat about 12 o'clock – 5/6d for myself and the dog. We were going on nice and we were passing a barge laden with malt for London. The Captain was an obliging man so he

[169]

called out, "I will tow you down the river" which, of course, all agreed to. I stopped up until 11 o'clock waiting for L. Lloyd, Esquire, but he did not come.'

> Two days later Llewellyn Lloyd arrived and the sea passage was arranged. There were a few days to while away before the ship sailed.

'This morning L. Lloyd and myself set off for a walk. He went to see the fort that I saw the other day. I stopped, talking to the sentry. He told me that the officers was devils. We stopped on a point of land that had command of the town and sea.

Thursday 5 of April 1837 at Harwich
This afternoon I was taking a trunk of L. Lloyd's Esquire into the boat to take it to the yacht. As I had it in my hands the boat gave way. I slipped with my right leg against the thwart of the boat. Hurt it very much – is very painful. Bandaged it well with brandy.'

> The next day, Larry was still complaining of the pain. Indeed, he was so concerned about it that he decided to seek further advice.

'I went to a doctor who told me that it was very bad cut. He gave me a bottle of lotion and twelve powders for which he charged ten shillings.'

> At last, after what was obviously a very tedious delay, they set sail on Tuesday 11 April 1837. The sea was rough with only one day of good weather throughout the voyage.

'Saturday 15 April
This was a fine day, so fine that I was able to go on deck. Wormed two dogs that was on board and the keeper that was going out to stop in Sweden wormed two more as I wanted to show him how to do it. This was the first amusement I had since I left my dear wife and children at Sheringham.'

Apart from being plagued as usual by sea sickness and by the constant pain in his leg, Larry's miseries were aggravated by the complete lack of provision for him on board the ship. This may have been through his own choice in an attempt to eke out his finances.

'Sunday 16 of April 1837 – on the sea
This day I was so ill that I could scarce look over my nose.

Monday 17 April
This day it blew a stiff gale. We could see the Danish coast which cheered

Llewellyn Lloyd, drawn by the Swedish courtier F. von Dardel, who also provided many of the illustrations for Lloyd's books.

us all up. I will never forget last night. I was so cold that I hardly could stand it as I had no berth in the ship, but lay on the boards in the men's cabins and my poor hip bones were so sore that I hardly could let my clothes touch them.

[171]

It was 11 o'clock in the forenoon that we saw the land. We ran 50 or perhaps 60 miles after that. As the ship was running at 9½ knots an hour, she struck on a rock. She fell to the wind. By that she kept upright. If she had fell the other way, we might be saved, but it would be so chancy as she would, most likely, filled with water.

Then, at about 8 o'clock, he hoisted a flag for a boat, but they were a long time before they came to us. Then they took us ashore up to the very small fishing town that I had visited the time I was in Sweden before. The men was pleased to see us there again.'

> The rest of the journey to Mr Lloyd's house was undertaken by road. Since 1831 he had been living in a large house at Ronnum on the southern shore of Lake Vänern. The two men stopped briefly in Gothenburg where Larry renewed his acquaintance with the Consul, Mr Harrison. He recorded in his diary, with sorrow, that the Consul's two daughters who had entertained him so well on his previous visit, had died of cholera in a virulent epidemic of the disease a few years before. Thankfully Larry and Llewellyn Lloyd reached the end of their journey on the evening of 20 April.

'This morning they brought me my breakfast to the bedside. It was bread and butter and plenty of coffee of the best. I got up, then went to Mr Lloyd's bedroom and there he was and on the bed there were a nice little girl about four years old. He was playing with it.

After this I went to see the birds. They are fine ones and I hope I shall have the honour to set them down in safety at Taymouth Castle.'

> The task of collecting the capercaillies together now became Larry's main preoccupation. Even before his arrival, word had been spread that capercaillies were wanted and a number of birds had already been assembled at Llewellyn Lloyd's house.

'This morning a man brought a fine cock to us. This is a fine bird. He came three miles – I mean Swedish miles, twenty-one English. This is a great way to bring a bird for 1/8d English money.

Mr Lloyd told me that he is to be hauled up for cutting so many of the forest trees for the birds to eat in the house that they are confined in. They eat the tops and barley and white peas, also wheat and drinks water.'

> It was imperative that the birds should be well housed in order that they should remain in prime condition.

Stalking Capercaillies in winter.
Llewellyn Lloyd's book *Game Birds and Wild Fowl of Sweden and Norway*, from which
this is taken, was published in 1867.

'Tuesday 25 April
This day Mr Lloyd set off to Trollhättan to get some boards for to make
coops. Two men came to make coops. They were making one coop nearly
one day. It was nearly 5½ feet long by 3 feet in breadth, 2½ feet high at the
back and 3½ high in front with a middle in it for to fasten the birds in one
while the other would be cleaned out on the sea . . . I got two of the coops
with a door so that I can take the birds out as I please by shutting one in at
a time which will be a great service to me on my travels.'

> After many complaints about the slowness of the workmen, a
> fortnight later Larry wrote with relief –

'The coops is finished at last.'

> Larry set about preparing the birds for their long journey with very
> great care. He felt that the responsibility for the enterprise lay
> entirely with him. He was also anxious that his success should
> reflect upon his master, Thomas Fowell Buxton, whose good name
> he was keen to promote at all times.

'The birds are to get used to me . . . We went to the wood and cut two alder
trees to make small troughs for the great birds to drink out of them. They

[173]

cut them out with a chisel. Each of us carried a piece of the tree . . . I made a trough of boards the same as they are made all over the world, but they seemed to wonder at it.

This day I set boughs in the house to make it appear dark as the birds is then quiet in the house.

Monday 29 May

Mr. Lloyd was well pleased to see the birds was home. He told me that his housekeeper did not like the system of my feeding my birds, but I ought to feed three times a day. I feed as they want it and every morning clean the dirt away, and clean water for them at different times in a day as I see needful. Now I shall state her system of feeding when they were under her care. They always had food, dirty or clean . . . and water the same and ne'er clean the house out of the dirt, only once a week. When I get it the thing is altered altogether. What a difference between doing and to tell people to do anything, but I take care of my birds without anyone to dictate for me.

Tuesday 30 May

At night I was surprised to find that the housekeeper was at Mr Lloyd to set to and remove the coops. I had them all in a row and plenty of boughs about them and I told Mr Lloyd to let well alone, which he agreed with me as the less all wild birds is disturbed the better for themselves.

I bought a bottle of brandy this day for 3½d. for to treat the men at the saw mill that used to give me the sawdust to keep the birds sweet and clean.

Sunday 4 June

This morning I was just after dressing my poor ill leg when Mr Lloyd called me as he generally do at an early hour each morning. I am glad to say that I am full as much engaged in the birds as he is. I am at their tails early each morning at about 5 sometimes, as I will get up to see if all is right with them sometimes at 4 o'clock, but still I must say I do not hold in disturbing them so often.

I left a hen in the coop in with the cock. They fought and she bled a good deal in the wings.'

Mr Buxton was kept in touch by letter with the progress of the enterprise.

'Thursday 18 May

A fine cock bird came to us this day. It is a tame one. It jumped on the perch when put into the coop. Its cost is now £5. What will it cost before it gets to the Highlands, if it ever do? This will cost T. F. Buxton, Esquire, £150 or

£200 to do it well. What a lot of money to spend after the great birds. Mr Lloyd is writing a letter to T. F. Buxton, Esquire, M.P., to inform him all about the birds which I think he is entitled to. At the same time I shall write a line to my wife and children to inform them how I am in this part . . . as they are at this present moment sitting down to tea at five or a little after.

Friday 19 May 1837
This day about 2 o'clock I had the pleasure of receiving a letter from my dear wife. Of course, it gave me great pleasure to find she was well and the dear children and all the neighbours, only James Parsons who fell from a horse and was not out of bed this last three weeks.'

> On this trip to Sweden, the diary reflected the changed relationship between Larry and Llewellyn Lloyd from that of the first visit. Larry is no longer Mr Lloyd's servant. It is clear that he had much more freedom and that although he often occupied himself with tasks for the household, he felt himself in no way bound to Mr Lloyd.

'Wednesday 10 of May
I was up at an early hour and as usual done all I had to do and as I was going out to fish, Mr L. said it was a great pity that I did not take another wash at his gig. It was dirty enough . . . I must say that Mr L. is in an ill skin this day, all about the bird that died . . . It seems to me that Mr Lloyd is ne'er satisfied unless he keeps all about him running about whether they have anything to do or not.'

> Larry's bad leg continued to be extremely painful and it was particularly troublesome when he walked for long distances.

'I showed my leg to Mr Lloyd who very coolly said there were nothing the matter with it and it would soon get well.

Sunday 4 June 1837
I called on a doctor to see what he would say about my leg. Here is all he said. He said wash it with cold water and put a plaster to it of this coarse-looking stuff that he gave me. Charged me about 2d. English money.'

> This treatment appears to have had little success and Larry continued to suffer pain and inconvenience with his leg.
> The diary shows that Larry had a good deal of free time in which to amuse himself.

'I had to climb up a steep hill or as I might term it a mountain of about 100 feet in height. The path was all rocks and the steps was all cut by nature that we had to contend with, but it was still of a beautiful sight to look back on the valley and fields and fine river that we just passed by and trod on its surface and at such an elevated site so that we could see for miles around.'

> At other times Larry fished, sometimes making a splendid catch of pike, salmon, sea trout, perch and other smaller fish. He used nets, lines and, on one occasion, joined an expedition to spear fish from a specially constructed boat with an iron platform fixed outside the prow on which a burning brand was fixed to attract fish at night.

'Wednesday 10 May 1837
After breakfast, I set off to the decoy where the fish was kept for bait with my arm striving to get some of them out. Then went up the river to fish. Got one salmon of 13 pounds – a fine fish it was. The day was cold. I again set out in the afternoon and killed another of 18½ pounds. This is a fine place to fish as any I ever was at . . . The water is so cold that the fish at its coming out is so cold that a person hardly could bear the cold of it.'

> True to his promise to the Buxton boys, Larry carefully collected together a variety of skins to take back to Norfolk.

'This day I got a great owl of the forest. The man says there is two more in his neighbourhood. I wish he may get it for me. I got a China duck. A fine bird it is. I am put into a room by myself to keep all my skins together. I have them all set up about the room. They looks well – five of the great birds, two of the duck species, two woodpeckers, one hawk, two blackgame, one owl – a fine bird – three other ducks, I know not what sort, two squirrels, one kittiwake of a large sort.'

> By the time of his departure from Sweden, he had added a number of other bird skins to his collection including a mallard, a red-throated diver, a plover, a black duck, a blackcap, two tree-creepers, a coot, a jay, two green woodpeckers, two black woodpeckers, sandpipers and various members of the crow family.
> Towards the end of May, Larry began to prepare the birds for their journey.

'22 May
The man came with the birds – five tjäders [capercaillies], three hens and

'A capercaillie cock and hen' by Archibald Thorburn.

[176]

Pl. 54

Capercaillie (&q)

two cocks. The man tells us that one of the cocks died on the road, but it is no odds for there is plenty of that sort at present. There is eleven cocks, fourteen hens. This is plenty to try what they will do in the Highlands if they arrive safe there as I trust in the Lord of all, for my sake that He through His goodness will let me have it to record that I was the bearer of them to that fine country.

I am by myself in my room thinking of my dear wife and children although far from me, but near in heart.

1 June

Mr Lloyd and myself carried the boards to the boat to make a platform for the coops to stand on. This way I could walk between them to feed and water them.

This day I found a hen tjäder half eaten by the rats. From her I took a full-grown egg, but this I shall tell to Mr Lloyd in the morning as he would be in a bad mind all night.

2 June

This morning I was up a little after 4 o'clock and tended all my birds. Then was called to speak to Mr L. The first word was, "How is the birds?" "One hen was dead and eat almost up by the rats." He said he was sorry for it as I truly say I was the same. I am to get poison for to kill the rats as there is no such things as small traps here . . .

Four gentlemen came to see the birds this evening . . . I got blinds of coarse cloth put up before all the coops the way that they will see no one on their way to Scotland.

Tuesday 6 June

The men is now at the boat getting it in order to take the birds down the river to Gothenburg at a moment's notice . . . Then we put all the birds on board and it was heavy wet so that it wet me right through. I got a cup of tea for all the night . . . then returned to the wet and cold.

Wednesday 7 June

This morning I rose from under the coops from my bed of damp straw that I lay like a wet dog. One o'clock at daybreak the hens began to fight so that I thought they would kill one another. In short, in this kind of rout they kept

'A view of Cromer' by James Stark, painted about 1835. Both steam and sailing ships can be seen in the distance.

'The vegetable market and Guildhall, Norwich' by D. Hodgson.

until 4 o'clock. I watered and fed them. The coops was all full of feathers and spotted with blood . . .

I went up to the house and got a cup of coffee and I am sorry to have it to say, this horrid temper returned to Mr Lloyd as he wanted to have the men there to start off at the hour he wished, but they were not of his mind. They never made their appearance until 9 o'clock . . . I am thankful to say we got out in the stream at a quarter past 2 o'clock and arrived to the town of Trollhätten in the dark.'

At Gothenburg, the birds were put aboard a brig.

'I went to the Custom House, got my pass and dined at the inn. Then went and got some boughs for my birds at a gentleman's not far from Gothenburg and he told me to come for as many as I liked.

I should like to go up to town to take something home with me to my wife and children if I can . . . I bought two caps to take with me to England as I want one of them for my son Samuel and I will wear the other . . . Mr Lloyd gave me the money it cost me for the caps.

Weighed anchor at 7 o'clock. The wind turned to the eastwards. It helped us to slip down the river. There is one of us glad to be on the way – it is myself . . . I am to give ten shillings to the crew at Hull if they behave well to me on my voyage.

Monday 12
There is a thick fog on the sea so that they are always blowing the horn . . . It put me in mind of the little boys in the woods blowing their horns to keep the wolves from the sheep and goats. They are made of wood, split and hollowed out then bound together. They are about four or five feet in length.

Thursday 15 of the month
One of the last wild cocks that I got was very ill. I feed it, but there is no hopes of it. It ne'er fed well and it was put in the coop with a tame one which was against it as the brute always beat it.

Monday 19 June
This morning I was called by the mate of the vessel to inform me that he could see the coast of Yorkshire. What a good news it was to me! The steamer sails every Wednesday from Hull to Dundee. I fear that I will not get in in time for it. The wind is all gone and the sea like a mill pond – not a ripple to be seen on it. The birds is all well at present which is a great blessing for me.

Tuesday 20 June
This morning they weighed anchor at an early hour. I came ashore into Hull where I bought two caps – one for one of the sailors and the other for myself. I wrote two letters – one for T. F. Buxton, the other for my wife.'

> The following day Larry went to the Customs' House in Hull to pay the dues for the passage of the birds. These amounted to £1. 2. 0. He then transferred the birds to the ship, the *Forfarshire* – a ship which was to spring to fame in the following year when Grace Darling and her father rowed out to save the crew.

'I must say that at home is the worst part that a man will be treated as I can truly say that the officers here in Hull take too much on themselves.'

> This part of the journey was accomplished quickly and the last stage of the mission was now in sight. He landed at Dundee on 22 June.

'Friday 23 June
I may say now I have in my purse £4. 5. 6., but I am in this country where they seems if they all would do anything to get the birds safe . . . They take charge of the birds and put a man over them and sent me up to Perth to get all things ready for me to start with the birds to Taymouth Castle in the morning.

At Dundee, there did a deal of all sorts come to see the strangers. There were two beautiful ladies and gentlemen come to see them . . .

They all was obliged to me for the sight of them, one only asked me to have a glass of ale which I did. I also gave all accounts of these birds to the Newspaper office and told the young man to return thanks to all the gentlemen of Dundee for their kindness to me.'

> As a result of Larry's interview with the reporter, the following article appeared in the local newspaper –

> > 'THE COCK OF THE WOOD – T. F. Buxton, Esq. MP has procured twenty-eight birds of the cock of the wood species, and brought them over to Britain. They were collected throughout Sweden, notices having been circulated in every district offering rewards for each living cock or hen which could be obtained. Mr Buxton has presented them to the Marquis of Breadalbane, Taymouth Castle, Perth. Twenty-nine were shipped, only one died on the passage. In plumage they resemble the black cock, but in size they far surpass. The cocks, when full grown, will average 16 pounds. They betrayed none of the trepidation and uneasiness

of wild birds of a less noble species. The cock of the wood, once the inhabitant of the pine forests and heath-clad hills, has long since disappeared from Scotland – the northern and most uncivilised portion of which was the last place in Britain where it was seen. In some countries on the Continent, especially Sweden, it continues to live free from molestation. The difficulty of penetrating to the retreats chosen instinctively by a bird of all others the most chary of connection with mankind, the delicacy of its flesh, and the symmetrical beauty of its form, rendered it a bird of great value.'

Interest in the birds was as keen at Perth as it had been at Dundee.

'Five carts took them up to my quarters. The whole city of Perth was all alive – the old and young of all sorts was crowding in the streets to see those birds. Some, of course, saw them, but not all as it would take a long time to permit all the favour . . . Now I have packed them all up in the small hampers that I brought from Sweden for that purpose. The hen that had her wing broke is still alive and looks happy. Now set off to the north with all the birds packed one atop of the other to give them air, but I thank heaven that there were a fine cool breeze . . . The good lady of the house where I started from let the horse and her vehicle go all the way to his Lordship's with me. That way I would not have to change the vehicle which is very good and kind of her to do.'

Despite all the publicity surrounding their arrival, it must have been bitterly disappointing for Larry to find that no adequate provision had been made for the capercaillies. Those arrangements which had been made showed that there was no understanding at all of what the birds would be like.

'Now at Taymouth Castle, 8 o'clock at night and to my great surprise there were not a bit of a place to put the birds in, but we put them into chicken coops and fitted them as well as we could. So I must say it was a great neglect of them not to have a house for them, but near half an acre paled in with pales of ten or fifteen feet high, but no net to stop them in. But there is a saw mill and plenty of men to do anything for me. On Monday if all is well I shall get a house made for them in all haste. I should like to see all things ready for my feathered family who was under my care for so long a time.

Monday 26 June

The house for the birds is getting on delightful. A few shillings worth of whiskey will do wonders in the North. But I am ashamed to say that some

Taymouth Castle, Perthshire, the seat of Lord Breadalbane. The Scots pines which cover
the encircling hills made it an ideal habitat for capercaillies.

of the birds' heads scarce has a feather on them as they are looking to get out
of their close confinement.

I am expecting a letter from T.F.B. Esquire, MP with some money in it
as I have not enough to take me home.

Wednesday 28 June
I had a fine view of the Lake Tay, also Ben Lawers, the third highest
mountain in Scotland. They showed me a valley to the south of this lake
where there is a hermit's cave. They say it is well worth a stranger's visit
which I mean to do before I leave.

This day I got a letter from T. F. Buxton, Esquire, MP with £10 in it,
also another from Ed. Buxton, Esquire telling me to go to the North to see
two moors that is to let for the season.'

Taymouth Castle fascinated Larry and he spent much time looking
at its treasures and curiosities.

'This day I took a small walk round the pleasure grounds and the gardens of
flowers. It is well worth the stranger's while to visit them as he will see all sorts
of pictures cut out of stone, first men and women in full size and all kinds of
beasts, and the flowers set in the midst of them to the best advantage . . .

I saw the armour in the castle and a few of the pictures and all other weapons of war that they used to fight with in old times in the North. There is one old man that told me they used to go to the small lords' houses or small castles and kill all and burn the castle and take the estate and cattle for the spoil for themselves. I also saw the shoes and long gloves they used to wear when they used to go on this dreadful work – the shoes to not make noise and the long gloves not to let the human blood stain the arms. I saw a cross bow. The stock of it is bone and the steel is of a great thickness so that I or two more like me could not set it. I ne'er saw a finer trigger in my life. Also the swords is of a great length and weight also. They used to wear at that time armour made like scales of fish and metal hats. By that the great men led the others to the slaughter.'

> At the beginning of July, Larry prepared to leave Taymouth, his task completed.

'I was sent for to Mr Woodley, the factor. He told me that his Lordship was so much obliged to my master, he was not aware of what he could do in return for him. But I said it was already done as his Lordship had done a very kind turn for my master and I was very happy to be the bearer of the birds to their native soil and I had no doubt but they will do well in the woods in this country. His Lordship sent to me a present of five pounds which, of course, I thought a nice thing of his Lordship to do . . .

Here is my departure from the castle at two o'clock. The mail cart came through this beautiful park for to sweep me away from this fine place where a man ought to think himself blessed to be allowed to live in.

Now the servants of the castle – all sexes – gave me three times three to cheer Poor Larry's heart. I was much obliged to them for all their kindness to me. The labouring men that was there also joined in the cheering for me which it was a great honour to pay to me an entire stranger to them all.'

> After travelling north to Inverness to inspect the game prospects of several moors for his master, Larry boarded the *Forfarshire* at Dundee, thankful that he was, at last, on the final stage of his journey home. The passage was a wretched one – the weather was wet and stormy and Larry was, of course, sea sick. By the evening of Thursday 20 July the ship was off the north Norfolk coast.

'We drifted with the tide down to Weybourne. Then about 11 o'clock we were against Sheringham where the Captain dropped anchor and at 12 o'clock I put my feet on the shore . . . I am sorry to say that a good many of the neighbours is dead. My dear wife and children is well which is a great blessing for me.'

——————⟨∘⟩⟩▱⟨⟨∘⟩——————

Chapter Thirteen

IN THE HIGHLANDS

1837

In spite of his long absence in Sweden, Larry was to have less than three weeks at home.

Immediately on his arrival, the young Buxton boys called at Larry's house to see the large collection of birds' skins he had brought back for them and he made arrangements to take them up to Northrepps.

'Tuesday 25 of July 1837

This morning I got my father-in-law's horse and Mrs Upcher's cart. Packed up all the skins, then set off to Beeston . . . then got to the Hall. My dear wife, dear boy was with me. They all were happy to see me there and was pleased to see the skins.'

The main topic of conversation at the Hall, however, was the forthcoming election to the first Parliament of Victoria's reign. Buxton was standing again at Weymouth, but with little hope of re-election.

'They tells me that for my master there is no chance of him being returned . . . Mrs Upcher thinks it all for the better. It may be so for what I know, but this I thinks, that there is honour attached if nothing else comes to the family.

Monday 31 of July 1837

This evening I went and saw Mrs Upcher. She had a letter from T. F. Buxton, Esq. and he mentioned that he was very thankful to have it to say he was not a Member any more which, if this gentleman will think so, it is all in his favour as his health is wearing fast and the man is of a great length. By that, he is more apt to fall to the ground in early life, but I wish it may not be the case with such a good-hearted man as T. F. Buxton, Esq. is.

Friday 4 August

This morning I saw Mrs Upcher again and she and I had rather a good deal to talk about and I was not ashamed to tell her that I felt rather hurt at the treatment that my master gave me last year and if it was a burden to his honour to keep me I should a thousand times rather that he would tell me to get a place as, at present, I was able and willing to work for my wages. I shall think of it all the days of my life. What she thought of it I know not and, at present, do not care a rap.'

> Larry visited many friends and acquaintances and caught up with the local news.

'I saw James Parsons at Mrs Upcher's. He took but little notice of me nor did he ever since my return from abroad, but that is no odds to me.'

> During his short respite at home, Larry was very busy. He worked in his garden, weeded the paths, made a garden seat 'for my dear wife to sit on when she finds a leisure hour'. He tied flies for the Buxton boys to take with them for fishing on their forthcoming holiday.

'They made me a present of a small spy glass. Suits my eyes well.'

> He also worked out his accounts and settled his bills. He was ready to travel north once again.
>
> Larry joined the Buxtons at Grassington in Yorkshire on 15 August after a tiring journey with many frustrating delays. In consequence, he recorded that he was not in the best of spirits when he met his master, but the gift of a knife and a copy of his farewell address to the voters of Weymouth soon restored his good humour. Larry wrote that he would keep the address all the days of his life.
>
> After a few days' sport at Grassington, the Buxton family moved on to Scotland for the main summer shooting. Larry set off separately to continue his journey to the Scottish moors by a very roundabout route, taking with him the dogs and the pony. He stopped first at Bury and then Manchester where he took the train to Liverpool.

'To the steamer train. Pony – his fare 9 shillings, dogs – 3 shillings, 4 shillings for myself. They tells me the distance is about 36 miles. Now in Liverpool. This distance we ran in 1 hour and 25 minutes. We passed through a tunnel of 1 mile and a ⅓ and 28 yards. It was a dismal sight to see the travellers when passing a light, just as if we were all lifeless corpses. It was as silent as the grave.'

Larry amused himself for the rest of the day by wandering round Liverpool's new market which interested him greatly. He also went to a prize-fight and saw the boxer John Langan, the former Irish champion. This boxer, Larry notes, had once fought the great Cribb. He had lost that particular fight, but on this occasion he was victorious, though there is no mention of the name of his opponent.

The following day Larry boarded the steamer and settled in the animals.

'I was waiting to start off to the stormy sea which at all times generally gives me a good cleaning out . . . I was on the deck and heard one of my dogs call out. It was from one of the sailors hit him with a rope which he was very near killing the poor dog.

Sunday 2 of this month

They were obliged to wait for the tide at Greenock where four or five of us went ashore. We got our breakfast for which each of us paid 1 shilling and 2d each for the waiter. A young woman about eighteen or thereabouts waited on us. She was pleasant looking, but she was a Tory . . .

Now up to Glasgow. A long time striving to get the vessel alongside of the quay to land all of us, but at last it was done, but a great bustle it made in the city.'

Glasgow, at the time Larry passed through en route to the Highlands.

The following morning, Larry unexpectedly spotted his master passing by in a post chaise. Buxton readily agreed to take Larry's luggage with him.

'I then got shaved by a barber and he told me the reason of them, some years ago, to put out a striped pole. It was they all bled people, but now they do not and the pole is hardly ever put up and at that time they also dressed all grievous wounds. But all that is done away with now as doctors was so ·plentiful.

It was raining fast at the time I started off . . . It came down as if it was coming out of a riddle. By that it wet me right through in the space of two or three miles. I went and took shelter in a house and dried myself. I paid eight pence to them for their kindness to me. Then set out again. Came to Dunbarton where I was last year. The good old fat Missis of the house was happy to see me. I think at the least she must weigh 17 or 18 stones – 14 pounds to the stone – She is a widow at this time which is a good thing for if she fell out with her husband whoever he might be, all she had to do to get rid of him was to lie on him at night and it would be all up with him in a very few minutes. But a civil lady to me and all things cheap and good is in her apartment – at least I found it the twice I called there.'

Two days later he joined the family who had arrived some days before him. Larry's dismal spirits returned at Dalmally – 'this dull place' he called it. The weather was extremely bad and he suffered from aches and pains as a result of repeated soakings by the heavy rain. Larry and his master were both unwell and Buxton's temper was as short as Larry's. An incident with a rogue, who took advantage of Buxton's gullible nature, caused Larry much annoyance and he complained at having to work so hard on top of a long day's shooting.

'Now after the sport of the day I had to tread the road home again by myself. I thought of thousands of things and my dear wife and children often comes to my mind, but if all is well I trust I shall live to see them all again. This month is at a close with many a weary step to my poor foot, also many a doleful sigh to my heart and damp to my spirits too, although I keep up my spirits before my masters and all others.

I have to clean all shoes, brush the clothes and take off my pony, dogs, guns and if I have not enough to do at this present time, I hardly know what is enough for a servant to have to do.'

[186]

The party moved on to Tyndrum. Game here was more plentiful and good shooting soon was well under way. Larry began to be more cheerful, although he did not care for the ladies' interest in shooting; however, it was an interest which was short-lived.

'The morning was beautiful for to behold as I came along, to see the sun shine in different parts of the hills as the cloud passed by. All the small farmers in the small floats gathering up the hay for their stock for the winter months and the shepherds rising up the sloping road with their flocks and a dog or two attending them, all add to the scenery.

I passed the right of a lake where Rob Roy's castle is in the middle of it. Also passed the remains of the house where he was born. It is only a chimney and a part of the end and side walls standing. They say that the estate owner will not allow it to be taken down.

30 August
This was a fine day and a finer ground I ne'er hunted in my life – 14 grouse, 5 blackgame, 1 wild-fowl, 2 snipe. One was a beauty of an old blackcock. I saw 6 or 7 old cocks. They looked beautiful flying across the deep black valley of Glen Dochart.

Friday 1 of September 1837
The keeper thought to get some shots at grouse just by the house . . . T. F. Buxton, Esquire, was so angry that he was out of temper all day and a plain proof it was the case, for he only bagged 5 grouse, 1 hare . . . I found 3 wounded birds this day by good marking . . . They gave me great credit as the keeper or men here ne'er think of such a thing as to take notice of them that fly away. At lunch I happened with a good fare. It was four boiled eggs which I liked well as they had plenty of meat . . . Also we had some of the whiskey which was very cheering although I ne'er take much at a time of it, but on the hills here some of it is wanting. I must say that T. F. Buxton, Esquire, took it rather freely as he could not shoot a bird.

Saturday 2 September
This morning we faced up the hills to the eastward of this inn and two ladies with us – Mrs N. Buxton and Miss Gurney, her sister. They stopped for a while. When they saw one poor creature lose its life, they returned to the inn. The fair sex is all very well in their proper place, but in the field of sport, I think it is not a proper place for them.'

[187]

Lord Breadalbane, on whose Taymouth estate T. F. Buxton and Larry introduced the capercaillies. From a drawing by G. Hayter.

The Buxtons and Larry then moved to Taymouth where they were the guests again of Lord Breadalbane. Each day was spent deer-stalking, a new sport for Larry. His overriding preoccupation was to ensure that his master killed a deer. This was a particularly difficult feat to accomplish as Buxton's agility seemed to be much reduced.

'We all faced up a hill. My master did a deal better in regard of creeping up this mountain than I thought he would, but not long until they called out all to sit still. I could not see the cause of the sudden halt, but they soon showed me the cause. It was some deer feeding . . . It was not long until the forester called out that "Here they comes". I must say at the time such a noise with hoof and horns I ne'er heard before and truly I may say such a grand sight I ne'er witnessed before, for I saw 200 of these noble animals come within forty or fifty paces of our very noses.

Up rises T. F. Buxton, Esquire, and fires into the cluster of those creatures, some of them a deal bigger than Norfolk donkeys and the fine little calves calling to their beloved mothers as they went up the mountain side . . . I was so sorry that my master did not kill one. Now comes the deer-stalking of what I often heard of and read a deal about. The forester took the lead. All followed him in what I call grave silence, for not a word was spoke, only by the move of the hand and look of the eyes, but at last we came within about eighty paces of this fine beast . . . T. F. Buxton, Esquire, fired at him. He hit his left horn about four inches above the head as I saw smoke out of it. I shall ne'er forget the leap that this animal took down the mountain side where the great rolling stones went at a tremendous pace.'

The following day's sport is described by Buxton himself in a letter to his sons.

'It was very wet and the hills covered with clouds. We went up a hill, the highest mountain hereabouts . . . It was raining and blowing hard all the time and I was very much blown on reaching it . . . Then I and Larry were ordered to lie down and be quite quiet in one place and Lord Dunmore and a Highlander in another. It was on the ridge of a hill – blowing and raining hard – very cold – and I wet through and through – and there we lay for two hours – "Oh, oh", said Larry in a whisper, "if the Missis could see us here – eight miles from the house, perched up a hill, with nothing to look at, but rocks and rain – how she would fret herself".

However, there was no help for it, so I amused myself by hearing Larry's stories, of which he has a rare collection – and by drinking a good lot of whiskey to keep the cold out – at last the other party arrived – and when I got up – for we had been lying down all the time, I could hardly stand for cold – but we were ordered off to another position, and a good walk over mountains, torrents and marshes soon brought us round. At the end of it we were very coolly ordered by his Lordship to go to the high point of another perpendicular hill – while he took his position about 200 yards below us – and Captain Murray 200 below him . . . After waiting some time a few deer passed us, out of shot . . .

The deer dogs were let loose. They singled out a buck and we ran down the hill as fast as we could – Larry screaming at me to take care . . . We ran then about two miles over a rough bog – the dogs every now and then bringing the deer to bay. It was a very exciting sport and wild enough. At length, just as it grew all but dark, Lord B. got a shot at him in the river – missed – another shot – and the stag fell dead . . .

So ends a day in which I have had as much exertion and as much danger as I wish for – in which I have been as much stiffened by cold and melted with heat and drenched by rain as I have any ambition for. Larry has just been in. I have read him this, with which he is much amused and says, "Ah, ah, it is well the Missis did not see your honour stuck up in that queer place on a hill – she would not have got over it for a month, that I know . . ."'

Larry, himself, added a postscript to the events of the day –

'His Lordship is to send the two haunches [of venison] to the present Queen, God bless her!'

Writing of the same day's hunting, Larry noted that at one point

'my master was obliged to give way as we were not able to assist this nobleman as fast as those others was able to go against the wind and rain coming in our teeth . . . T.F.B. was not able to contend with the hill . . . When I was helping my master, I have often heard his noble heart beat with the work of going up the slope.'

After another week of shooting, Buxton told Larry he would be leaving Taymouth the following week for Perth, then Dundee where they would set sail for Hull. Larry was very thankful for the prospect of an imminent return home and wrote 'I am near tired of the North.'

To Larry's great pleasure, it was during that final week that his master at last shot a deer.

'The keeper was willing to strive to get a shot for T. F. Buxton, Esquire, and off we went and drove a few of the small woods, but no deer . . . then the keeper went to a rising hill and saw a roe . . . Then we set off to get a shot at him and he was in an oat field and my master shot it and I had at last the honour of cutting the throat of him of my master's shooting. He was a fine little fellow, fine horns.'

At this point in the diary there is a sudden gap of four years. It comes at the end of Volume III where the last entry ends in the middle of a sentence. Careful examination of the pages shows that the last quire of paper in the book is very incomplete. All the volumes have been rebound in fairly recent times so it seems likely that the back of the volume in its original binding had become damaged and the final pages lost.

Chapter Fourteen

THE TOLL
OF THE YEARS

1841–42

When the narrative begins again in Volume IV, the Buxton family and Larry are again in Scotland deer-stalking in the autumn of 1841. They are far more successful than on the previous trip and many deer fall to their rifles. It is obvious that Buxton's health has declined considerably in the intervening years and Larry often has to support his master on the journey home.

Larry was extremely proud of his prowess as a deer-stalker; he was successful in spite of mist, bogs and repeated soakings – on one occasion, he and Edward North Buxton advanced on a deer by wading waist-deep along a burn and on another memorable day the Buxton party, aided by Larry, shot four deer. Buxton wrote of that feat to his sons Fowell and Charles.

'We are masters of four bucks! One gentleman who was here 3 years ago obtained great renown for having killed one – and we are at the very pinnacle of glory. Edward says that Larry has actually grown a foot in height and he is both proud enough and pleased enough. He says that now that his master has actually shot a deer, he doesn't care what happens.'

Even the ladies were enthusiastic when a deer was killed –

'I shall ne'er forget the sight of seeing the eyes of the ladies all sparkling the same as stars of a frosty night,' wrote Larry.

The shooting party was often accompanied by a shepherd and on one occasion Larry was too weary to walk home and spent the night with him.

The Liverpool–Manchester Railway on which Larry travelled with pony and dogs in 1837. The tunnel under Liverpool was an attraction for large crowds who paid one shilling each to see it.

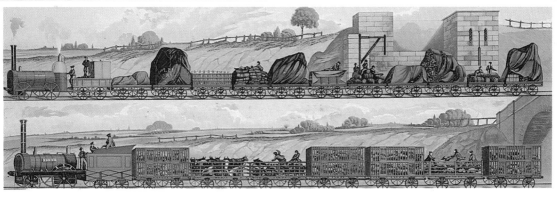

'Now the gents got their ponies and set off for home – about eight miles. Brown, the shepherd, and Poor Larry set off to the shepherd's house where the following live animals was keeped. There were the man and wife and his four children, seven dogs, one pig, two fat sheep, three cows – all of us to pig in the same apartment . . . the food we got to eat for the night is as follows – soup, potatoes, tea, barley and pea bread for which I may say that I was well satisfied with it as I would rather lodge here than walk eight miles to get a good supper.'

> Towards the end of September, the party broke up and Larry, together with the pony and six dogs took the steamer at Wick. He was lucky enough to have the dogs and luggage taken ashore by small boat at Overstrand, but as the pony could not be trusted to a small boat, Larry was forced to continue round to Yarmouth.

A good deal had happened during those four years now missing from the diary. The Banvilles had moved from Sheringham Lodge to a small house at Northrepps; James Parsons had left the service of the Buxtons, but his brother William was working at the Hall. Then in the summer of 1838, Larry had been sent to Sweden once again for a further supply of capercaillies. He brought twenty birds back with him, delivering sixteen hens to James Guthrie at Taymouth while the remainder went with him to Norfolk.

In 1840 the Prime Minister, Lord John Russell, had offered Buxton a baronetcy and, after a certain amount of family discussion, it had been accepted. Priscilla Johnston wrote at this time –

> 'My father's mind was very interesting. "I should like", he said, "very well to leave a strong anti-slavery, anti-slave-trade memorial to my family, otherwise it is little to me, only to call Hannah 'my Lady', that I should like."'

Larry clearly was proud of the title and took care always to write 'Sir Fowell' or 'Sir T. F. Buxton Bart'. However, years of overwork

Typical deer-stalking country in the Highlands of the 19th century. Artist unknown.
'Windsor Castle from St Leonard's Hill,' 1839 where Larry was sent with three capercaillies for Prince Albert, by C. R. Stanley.

had seriously undermined Buxton's health and he gave his family and doctors a great deal of worry. Larry's other master, Samuel Hoare, was also in declining health, being partially crippled. Larry did what he could to make sport possible for the two 'old gentlemen'.

'Saturday 25 of September 1841

This morning I set off to meet Mr Hoare. He can not shoot, but go to look on as he rides around after the gentlemen . . . S. Hoare asked me a deal of questions all about the sport in the North and said we made a deal of to do about the deer, but he would as soon eat a bit of a donkey. I would partly agree with my honoured master for I hardly can touch it as for eating it. I should not think it a bit of trouble to travel to the North to see my master shoot one every year of his future life and wish it might be twenty years longer . . . I fear very much that this will be the last visit with my master to the North. May the Lord spare him for years to come, but he wears fast at present.

'The Shooting Party', an engraving by J. H. Engleheart from a painting by A. Cooper. 'I had to carry all the game. Broke my harness. It was a bad thing to have all to carry on my small pony.'

Rabbit-shooting. Re-loading muzzle-loaders would certainly seem an irksome exercise today but no doubt loaders became swift and proficient, like the man on the hill.

Saturday 9 of October

Sir T. F. Buxton, Baronet, could not shoot at all. He shot 3 snipes. Then went off home which was the best thing he could do as he appeared not well.

Wednesday 3 of November

This was a fine day. They shot at Weybourne Hills – five guns. The game is as follows – 2 partridges, 5 pheasants, 1 wildfowl, 53 hares, 18 rabbits. This makes it 79 total. I waited on Sir F. and had to drag him up the hills the same as in Caithness. He shot well. I had to carry all the game. Broke my harness. It was a bad thing to have all to carry on my small pony.

Saturday 27 November

I was at the Hall the most of the day, but it was not fit to hardly turn a dog out of doors, but still it was a wonder for no weather seems to stop Mr Hoare although in such a feeble state as he now is, hardly fit to walk not to talk of shooting.'

Sir Fowell was well enough to address the farmers at their 1842 New Year dinner.

[195]

'Friday 7 January

We set out to shoot. They shot across Northrepps and nearly to Southrepps, then nearly to the bounds of Sidestrand. What game was bagged is as follows – 4 partridges, 1 rabbit, 1 woodcock. What a lot of game to get after walking full 9 or 10 miles nearly up to the knees in snow and slush! I must say I was sick of it.

Now comes 4 o'clock and the farmers came to dinner as they were to dine in the parlour with Sir T. F. Buxton, Baronet, T. F. Buxton and C. Buxton. They had all sorts for dinner – fish soup and 2 roasted geese, 1 turkey of a great size, a round of beef of 6 or 7 stone. After they were done it came to the keepers and we gave justice to it as it was as fine beef as I ever ate. I had the honour to help serve the beef. My dinner was fish and tarts as it was a day I do not use fleshmeats. They all seemed to spend a merry evening of it. Here is what the honourable Bart told the farmers – it is as follows: he would wish to have good dykes for his partridges, also to plant trees and furze in them. Bad farmers he would not have and good farmers he would not break.

Now comes his orders to the keepers. It is as follows as I wrote it down. "A man of mine that keeps a great store of rabbits or rats I shall not keep him." I was glad to hear him make the remark as they all well know that Sharmon Payne keeps plenty of rabbits and kills them for himself and makes the farmers pay for the rats.'

> Platten, the keeper at Beeston, was no better, a 'blackguard',
> 'half-witted' and quite untrustworthy.

'Came into the street. Saw Tom Platten there drunk and he told me not to come to shoot on his manor any more as a poacher and that Mr Hoare told him I had no right to shoot there. But when I am sent, I go and no other time to shoot. I am right when I am ordered by my master. This poor stupid man may thank me for the place he holds.'

> Larry had often enjoyed a good day's sport with James Parsons in
> spite of his faults, but he had little in common with men such as
> Payne and Platten. Banville had no manor of his own at this time,
> but he was kept very busy as personal attendant to Sir Fowell when
> he went shooting and kept a general eye on his master's interests.

'I saw five women leaving the plantation where they were at work taking up parsnips. In the first place they did not work their proper hours and at least they had a bushel and a half of the parsnips. When they saw that I was coming to meet them, they all threw them down the cliff. I shall tell Sir T.F. of it as I would not do my duty to my master unless I told him of it.'

Sir Fowell had become very interested in establishing plantations of trees and had bought land at Runton and Trimingham for conversion to forest land. Larry was closely involved in these new undertakings. There was a steady stream of visitors to view these plantations and the custom was for members of the family and other well-wishers to plant trees in prominent positions. The plantations provided much-needed employment for the Norfolk men,

'Friday 21 January 1842
Set off on the carriage box to Trimingham with Sir F. Buxton, Bart. and Mr Clowes. They saw the plantations which they liked well. Mr Warnes of this parish came and told Sir Fowell Buxton that the men were not satisfied with the work as they do not earn enough to get a day's wages, but this I do not mind.

Saturday 22 January 1842
This morning I set off to Bodham. I fired 16 shots – 10 partridges. Three of those shots I missed as my fingers was so cold I hardly could feel the trigger. I hardly ever saw the gates of the fields covered with a sheet of ice before. The young blades of wheat was froze the size of a reed in some of the fields that I crossed, also so slippery that I hardly could walk across them. It snowed on me the most of the way home. My coat was white.

I was speaking to Sir Fowell for a good while. He is thinking of another plantation at Trimingham as the poor want work, but he will not please all as he cannot keep them all at work, but it is good for all that, as it will make room for others.

. . . Here is a thing that Payne asked me to do for a man of the name of Tom Smith – to let him get work in the plantations. This is the man who took another man's wife away and left his own wife to starve or go to the parish. His wife sold all she had to live on. I shall tell Sir F. about it then let him do as he please.

Saturday 5 March
This morning I set off to Thorpe [Market], then to Southrepps, then to the Hall where I found Miss Buxton and C. Gurney going in with Sir T. F. Buxton, Bart. to Runton to see the plantations. The fair ladies planted a silver tree apiece in the top of the Niger plantation, one at the south and the other to the north of the road or ride that is left for shooting. What creatures

they were to handle a plant or a spade! If they were no other use than that what would become of them?

Wednesday 9 March

I fed the pheasants then I went up to the Hall as they were to plough up the field at the Hall for the nursery. I packed up 13000 [sic] trees for the plantation.'

> Larry seems to have turned his hand adeptly to other tasks. On one occasion he was asked to kill a horse; and, using the training given him by a London hairdresser when he was first employed by Mr Lloyd, was sent for when a barber was needed –

'I dressed my two young masters' hair and they looked well. I cut three men's hair this day.

. . . This morning I went to Mrs Upcher's free school. I trimmed a deal of children's hair.'

> He also acted as a chiropodist –

'I went down to Lower Sheringham and waited on Mr Burcham. I cleaned his feet well, also dressed his corns and he told me that he did not go so easy for several years.'

> Larry and Mr Burcham became good friends and he dressed his corns over a period of ten years up to the time of his death.

'Saturday 2 October 1841

I must say that Mr Burcham of Sheringham was a worthy friend of mine for years before God took him. It is strange to say that all the time that he was on his death bed he had a wish to see me, but they did not let me know. If they had I should went to see him, but it is strange to say that he departed at 12 o'clock in the night and I was just lying down at that time. My wife was asleep. Three raps was made at my door as plain as anyone ever heard. It was so plain that I put my hand under my head to see anyone that would come up the staircase. I often heard that the house was haunted and that was the reason that I was willing to watch the door, but nothing came up that I could see.'

> In March 1842, the news came of the death of Mr Mark Lloyd, Llewellyn Lloyd's brother, for whom Larry had always felt so much affection. A few days later –

'I met Mr Tucker of Cromer. He was riding and he looked very ill indeed. I asked him for his health. "Very ill" was his answer. I said "Go home, Sir, and rest", but his answer was, "I cannot live without air."

Saturday 7

. . . I am sorry to relate it that Mr. Tucker that I spoke to yesterday was found dead in his bed this morning. Ah, may this be a warning for me and all to make ready for the call when it is made.'

Then on 9 March

'I got a letter from J. William Goff to inform me of the death of my dear father. I trust in the Lord of all that He took his soul to Himself.'

As an Irishman in Norfolk Larry still found his religion created controversy.

'This day as I was waiting for the parson, there were a few of the farmers that know all things began to tell me all about the Catholic priests – how they would forgive a man when he would kill another. But it is not the case. I told them as follows: they all ought to read the word of God and practise it, but it was not the case with them. They kept the Bible in their house, but done very little with it. If they did, it would not be the case with them to be always finding fault with the Catholics. I asked them the sins of Catholics, but not one of them could tell me.'

Everything seemed to be against him that winter.

'I put on a coat that a tailor made me, but it is too small for me – a great pity as I bought the cloth at Wick in Caithness when shooting, a present from Sir T. F. Buxton. I am much obliged to him for it and am much disappointed at it being spoiled by a Norfolk tailor.

. . . I lost my knife that Sir T. F. Buxton, Bart. gave me. I would sooner have lost 5 shillings, but I hope I shall get it again as my name is on it.

. . . I drank a horn of porter at Frank Abbs' of Runton and Sir F. saw it by me. Others would drink a gallon but no notice taken of it.'

Banville was also worried about the scarcity of pheasants. The poor gamekeeping in the shooting grounds during Larry's absences from Norfolk had resulted in a shortage of birds.

'Wednesday 17 November 1841

This day they shot through my covert and I can truly say it was a day of sorrow to me more than pleasure. The reason was because there were not many pheasants there. The reason was I gave all my young pheasants to my fellow-keepers by the order of my master, then was away two months. Besides this, I am always out with my master which is a bad thing for any keeper to be off his ground, but still my master is well satisfied – 4 partridges, 17 pheasants, 12 woodcocks, 31 hares, 18 rabbits. I was not in a good mind all day.

Monday 9 May 1842

This was the first time for me to be aware of losing pheasants' eggs. A man stopping gaps found it and that two men walked to the nest right through two fields, but it is hard to lay it to anyone.

Tuesday 10

I walked all round to all parts of my ground in a wretched mind about my pheasants' eggs . . .

Sunday 15

I set off to watch the fields and saw two boys after the eggs, but one I got. The father told me that if the keepers did not buy the eggs the boys would not steal them.'

In order to improve matters and so ensure a good season's shooting, a concerted effort was made on all the manors to rear more birds.

'Wednesday 18 May

I set off to the mill that grinds bones with a cart full. After that I set off to Scottow Hall, the seat of Sir Henry Durrant. The keeper was coming to me with 70 pheasants' eggs. I left him 28 ring-necked eggs.'

'The post-mill at Sheringham' by Henry Bright.

Overleaf: 'A covey of partridges in the snow' by Archibald Thorburn.

Hares were numerous and many were bagged: on 3 November 1841, 53 were shot at Weybourne Hills. This painting of the common hare is by Archibald Thornburn.

'Still Life' by Emily Stannard, 1853. Emily was the best painter of dead game in the Stannard family. Apart from the hare, this fine oil painting of a game shop in Norwich includes teal, woodpigeon, presumably grey plovers, a robin and possibly a greenfinch or a siskin. The plumage of the female teal and the two plovers looks inaccurate, but maybe Miss Stannard had to throw out the corpses long before she started painting those three. It is curious that such pictures so often included small birds like finches, but a robin is unusual.

Deer in the coverts, presumably escaped from Gunton Park, caused some excitement that summer.

'Wednesday 6 July 1842

This was a fine day. My man saw a deer in the covert. I set off to the Hall. Then Sir T. F. Buxton and Mr. Gurney came to see if we could kill it, but it set off in good style. I fired two shots at it as it galloped away, then I set off after him again. William Parsons fired two shots at him. Blood was on his footmarks, but we did not get him.

Monday 9 August 1842

This was a fine day and Mr Cheston came and told me a deer was in his wheat field. I went with my gun and dog and I saw him. He got up and walked a few paces clipping the ears of wheat at every step. I set off in the line where he was going and just as I put up my head to see if I could see the beast, he stood at the other side of the dyke, face to face. He made a leap of 4 or 5 yards, stood to look at me as he only could get sight of my face at first. I caught sight of about 4 inches of the deer, right between the thorn bulls. Now is my time. I fired at it and the ball hit him in the back just where they cut off the haunch of venison, but that was only chance as I could not tell what part I saw at the time I pulled the trigger, but got the beast. Its weight was 7 stone 5 lbs.'

A deer in a wheat field was fair game, but Larry did not think much of the London method of shooting deer.

'I went to Gunton Park to see the deer shot by a man from London. I went to see if I could find out how he shot the deer. It is as follows. The man gets up in a tree and there stops like a thief in the dark. There is men to walk the deer and let them stop about the tree where he is up in. By that he shoots them right through the head. He shoots the deer in Hyde Park at London. He may be a good deer shot, but he is one of the most ill-looking blackguards I ever saw.'

'Hannah, Lady Buxton' in later years, by George Richmond. She lived on at Northrepps after Thomas Fowell's death, corresponding regularly with her large family of children and grandchildren. She died in March 1872 aged 88. Only one of her children, Thomas Fowell the younger, survived her.

> Larry was also kept very busy at home. His house was not large
> enough for the growing family.

'Friday 11 February 1842

I set off to the head carpenter's. He told me it would cost £10. 9s. 3d. to
raise the roof of my little house. That way I would have two small bedrooms
above stairs. I agreed with Mr Martins for a few oak trees.'

> The work was soon finished and Larry whitewashed the new rooms
> and moved beds in. Meanwhile Larry and Sarah were thinking
> about Samuel's future.

'I went to Southrepps to speak about my son as he wishes to be a carpenter.'

> Perhaps the boy's interest had been kindled by the work on the
> house.

> Domestic details attracted Larry's attention during that hot summer.

'Friday 3 June 1842

A good many of the children of the parish was at mine. My wife tired and
ill-tempered. There were fifteen of the children. One cut its finger nearly
through.

Sunday 12 June 1842

I stopped at home. My wife went to church. I walked off to meet her and lay
or sat. By that I fell asleep. My wife came. Did not speak to me until she got
over it.

Sunday 17 July 1842

I was not very well this day. I took a small walk about my coverts. My wife
was in an ill skin for me to do that when I was not well enough to go to
church.'

> Then, at the end of August Larry wrote –

'I went to church, but my child came for me. I went home as fast as I could.
I found my dear wife not so ill as I thought. Forgot tea.

Monday 30 of the month

My dear wife was as bad as she well could be all day. The doctor stopped all
day with us. I may say that it was a day of trial.

Tuesday 31

This morning I set off to North Walsham for another doctor of the name of

Mr Beacon who came in quick after me. I am happy to say he was not wanting as my dear wife was confined of a fine boy a quarter before 3 o'clock this morning.'

This was Larry and Sarah's eighth child; his name was Henry.

During the months that followed, the health of Banville's masters did not improve. Both suffered strokes, but whereas Sam Hoare recovered some of his vitality in spite of a partially paralysed arm, Sir Fowell's health deteriorated.

'This morning I went out and shot a small hare, took it to the Hall, then went to Cromer. Got the pony shod there. I went to Clapham Dams with Lady Buxton and Sir F. He walked a little. He appears as weak as a cat . . . I fear that Sir F. will not be here long. What a day that will be to me I am not able to say. I may say that on that day I shall lose my earthly father in Norfolk.

4 November 1842
This morning S. Hoare Esq. shot a hen pheasant at 65 paces all with a single gun. What a thing to see the old sportsman shoot with one hand as the other is no use to him.

I am sorry to say that Sir T. F. Buxton Bart. is very ill, so ill that he cannot go out shooting.

Tueday 8 November 1842
This morning I set off to the Hall. There got orders to start off to Runton. They shot through the coverts – 48 pheasants. It was rather hard work for me to help Sir T. F. Buxton Bart. up the valleys, but all I can do I don't repent for it as, take him with his faults, he is the best of masters.

Chapter Fifteen

AN IRISHMAN AMONG WOLVES

1843–44

After an unexplained gap in entries for the second half of December, January 1843 was uneventful. But there are again no entries at all for the first seventeen days of February. It is not that the pages have been torn from the diary as in some previous instances. Banville simply did not record the events of those days.

On 31 January, Sir Fowell and Lady Buxton went to Windsor for an interview with Prince Albert about the failed expedition to the Niger in which Buxton had been deeply involved. Its aim had been to explore the area of the river, develop its agricultural potential and establish Christian missions; its failure struck him very deeply. 'They ended the interview', wrote Lady Buxton to her daughter, Priscilla, 'with a few words on shooting, and Prince Albert said he had been shooting your father's capercaillies at Taymouth. He offered to give him two tame ones, which quite pleased the Prince'. The breeding birds brought back by Larry in 1838 were in coops at Northrepps but sometimes escaped.

'Friday 20 January 1843
This day we shot at Gurney Hills where we saw a capercaillie hen in the wood. It flew out of the Scotch fir tree as they all do in Sweden. It got out of the house that we put it in. Sir T. F. Buxton Bart. was in the act of putting his gun up when I called out "A grey hen or capercaillie hen!"'

In late February, Larry was sent to Windsor Castle with two hens and a cock bird for Prince Albert.

'This morning I set off to the Hall. Then I got the capercaillies and took them home to my house. I then went to Roughton and set off to Norwich and from there to London. I got off and set off to the train at Paddington, then to

The equestrian statue of George III in Windsor Great Park, about which Larry observed
'they forgot to put stirrups on'.

Slough, then to Windsor. There got a bit of breakfast. I got my hair cut at Windsor, then to Virginia Water. I got a cab and drove off through the Great Park. I here saw the finest trees that I ever saw in my life. Saw a few deer. The distance is about 7 miles.

I saw the statue of King George. They forgot to put stirrups on which makes it look bad in my sight. Before the horse was put up, eleven great squires took breakfast in the body of it. The great mass of stone that the statue stands on is of a grey colour.

The horse and gig cost 7 shillings, the driver 2/6. I arrived at Virginia about 11 o'clock, morning cold. I put plenty of Scotch fir boughs in the baskets for the birds to eat which they took freely as they were very hungry I make no doubt. This is a nice place. I went up to the top of a hill. It was a fine view all round, 62 steps, each step 14 inches in height. I cut the form of my right foot and my name on it and the date of the year.

I left my name in the house as they wished it of me. The Prince's spaniels was here. They were in such a state . . . I ne'er saw dogs in such a state only at Col. Murray's in Scotland when I was at Gatehouse . . . They ought to have more room for a yard and some of the yard to be grass . . . They say those creatures have rheumatic pains. The keeper would have the same himself if he was shut up in his wet clothes and a damp bed. See whether this treatment would do long for him!

Saturday 25
This morning I got up, set off with Mr. Tanner with the birds to where they were to be kept. I must say it is a fine forest for game of all sorts, blackgame and those fine birds. I wish him luck with the capercaillies.

I then returned to London. The coachman was as merry a fellow as I have travelled with for many a day. Came in at 7 o'clock at Norwich.

'Monday 27 of March
This morning I went up to the Hall where I saw Sir T.F.B., Bart., but I truly must say that I ne'er thought a short time ago that I could hold him with such disdain . . . I set off to Beeston. Shot 3 rabbits, 1 snipe, 1 woodcock, but in fact I hardly cared whether I pulled the trigger or not. Day cold. My heart was cold, too, all day.'

> Exactly what had happened to alter so radically Larry's view of his master is obscure. It would appear that his crime consisted in listening to and believing some calumny against Larry reported to him by Mr John Cross, a Northrepps farmer, and others. It seems that both his drinking habits and his religion were involved and on his return from Windsor his deep resentment began to overflow into the pages of the diary.

'I am an Irishman and a Catholic into the bargain. Now I ne'er thought that a man of such a noble mind as my master is should think of upbraiding me for my way of believing in Christ . . . This hurted me so much that if I was at this time as I was when I first saw Sir T. F. Buxton, Bart., I should have taken my flight ne'er to return to his service again.

> Some weeks earlier Buxton had made Larry a present of a gun to keep until the time that Buxton might see him drunk.

'He was told I was often so, but it is all safe of my side in that affair, for I shall ne'er drink a drop of his ale or porter, so by that the gun will remain mine.'

> However, Larry found that such a vow was not easy to keep and that abstinence did not agree with him.

Friday 7 of April
This day I was as weak and ill as I have been for a long time. I drank nothing

only milk and water or tea from the first of March . . . My drink used to be beer and nothing else.

Saturday 8 April
I happened to meet William Parsons who told me that Sir T. F. Buxton, Bart. asked him if I was tipsy at the party. He told him no one was the worse for liquor and told him I ne'er was the worse for drink when he saw me and always the best company. Then said Sir F. "What did Larry say when he drank my health?" "Why, Sir, he told us all that he was in just the same form as an Englishman and that they all was well aware that when they crossed a field of a downy morning that if they trod on a worm it would turn on them. He was the same as that – if he was to be trod on he would do the same. He was pleased to do his duty in his place, but before he should give way without proper cause, he would suffer to be torn between wild horses. Then he told them that he hoped to meet them one and all with the same cheerful face as he hitherto had did and he hoped they would have better sport for the time to come and that his most noble master might live for many days in the parish."

Wednesday 12 April
This morning I went up to the Hall and there spoke to Sir F. and I asked to return home again as I was to meet Mr Peters [valet at Gunton Hall] and I did.

He told me that he ne'er heard anyone say such a thing of me in his life, and he wondered that Sir T. F. Buxton, Bart. would hear what such a man as Cross or Sutton had to say of his servant that served him so long and travelled thousands of miles in his service. He was ashamed to hear of it in the country where Sir T. F. Buxton, Bart. bore such a name as he do through town and country, and if I required a letter or a word he was willing to give either to me. What a good thing it was of him to offer to a poor Irishman in the middle of wolves.'

Another friend to stand up for Larry during that troubled spring was a neighbour called Thomas Curtis.

'Wednesday 15 March
Mr Thomas Curtis of Windspurs Farm spoke to Sir T. F. Buxton. He told this nobleman that I was now the same as when I first went under his roof and wished that he would let me stop with him, but the answer was he wanted me on his own ground.

[207]

Monday 20 March

This morning we set off riding, 10 of us in the party . . . John Cross of Northrepps was with us who is the biggest devil in the world. I am sure if Sir T. F. Buxton knew this man's account of him he would ne'er speak to him on any account. John Cross was made pay £10 for being with a woman of the name of Mrs Amis of Northrepps. He also wet hay and sold it by weight . . . but Sir T. F. Buxton Bart.'s eyes is not opened yet.

Monday 3 of April

I went up to the Hall. I there saw Sir F. Buxton and he told me to get a good big coat for myself. What will John Cross and his party of thieves say to that?

Sunday 9 of the month

I went to church with the big coat on and after service I spoke to Sir F. and thanked him for it. He hoped it was a good one. It cost £3. It looks well. Cold day.'

> As a final indignity the Banvilles were forced to move from Sheringham, to a house in Springdale Valley, Runton.

Tuesday 14 March

. . . I took my wife to the house, but she do not like it.

Wednesday 29

I went to Runton to fix my hen house. My saw was a bad one and that was not a good thing for to saw green boards. I also fixed a house for a hive of bees.

Tuesday 4 April

I set off to Beeston. I saw plenty of snipe. They were as wild as needful. I killed seven snipe and it turned to wet and I got a wetting in the bargain. I rode home wet through. On my way I called at the house at Runton. The bricklayers was at it. I gave them a shilling to drink as I wanted the house done as fast as they could.

Thursday 20 of this month

The first thing was to load Mr Thomas Curtis's wain with my furniture and sent it off to Runton. Then got all things ready to start. Then sent my children Charles and Elizabeth to go with them, but it happened that when we were going to start, it came a thunder storm and hail stones fell so big as I ne'er witnessed before. They were as big as marbles. When my brother-in-law was passing a house in Cromer and the hail fell on him he thought a friend was throwing stones at him. When we were driving up through the sandy pightle [a small irregularly-shaped field], Mr Curtis's pony checked, fell and broke the two shafts of the gig that had Mr Curtis and my dear sister-in-law Catherine Lown and my daughter Biddy, but they got no hurt which was a great blessing that they were not smashed. It was almost a wonder that they got out of it so well. My dear wife was with her young child in her arms with me – all of us in a fright and shall think of it all the days of our lives.'

> The occupants of the other half of the house, Mr and Mrs May, were not to the Banvilles' liking.

'Friday 21 April – Runton, Springdale
Not settled in it as all seems to be in a litter and all things seems strange to me at present. I think that the neighbours that is in the house, I shall not like, at least the woman, but it is to prove yet.'

> With the Banvilles living in such close proximity to the Mays, it was impossible for them not to notice the loose morals of Mrs May. Larry had always been very strict in his attitude to sexual licence.

'There is two men that is at work for Sir F. that goes to May's house when they can to clean harness, shoes and chop sticks. As the men that is at work with them says, "There goes the two parish bulls to Mrs. May."

Tuesday 24 May
Mr Johnson of Runton came up with a party. He took the party all in to May's. What a fine thing for the ladies to pay a visit to the biggest whore in Norfolk as we all know it.'

> It seems to have been common knowledge that Mrs May was Mr Johnson's mistress. The previous keeper to live in the Runton house had complained about it to Larry the year previously and now Larry and Sarah could not help but be aware of the goings-on next door.

'. . . I saw him [Johnson] met by Mrs May at her door half naked and her hair all about her naked breast – a shame to see it.'

> There was worse to come.
> In the meantime, Larry had to suffer the mortification of hearing a complaint about his son, Samuel, who was employed at the Hall.

'Sir F. told me that [some] one told him that my boy was not obliging at the Hall. I said I was sorry for that, but there is two gardeners at the Hall and Gray asked this son of mine when he was laying the cloth for dinner last

Sunday and all his clothes on ready to wait at table, this gardener that I mentioned asked the boy to go to feed the calf with him and the boy told him he was dressed to wait dinner and it would spoil his clothes. There was a fine thing to tell a gentlemen about!'

> To his indignation with people was added concern about his pheasants.

'Friday 9 June 1843

Up early and off to the coops, a dreadful sight to see as it was raining so fast it was enough to kill the little creatures if they put their heads out of the coops.

22 June

This was a doleful day for me as my young pheasants is dying as fast as they well can, from what reason I know not, the same as if they were poisoned by the human hand. The boy that I have do not attend to them when I am out. If I am spared to rear pheasants again, no one shall feed them but myself. A bad time for game of all sorts this season. I may say that all striving to get game this season will avail nothing, as I hear from all quarters complaints about them.

It is, I fear, all up . . . It has been one of the coldest springs that I witnessed for many a year. All the keepers told me the same that have wrote to me from north to the south, also from Ireland and Scotland.

12 July

My young golden pheasants are dead . . .

8 August

I went to Payne, the keeper at Hungry Hills to get some young pheasants by Sir T.F.B.'s orders, but he gave me 15 and a hard task it was to get them. I shall state what I gave him in two seasons – 52 one year and 60 another, then 15 was all he could give the poor Irishman. Mr. Took of Felthorpe told me he would like to give me 20 – that is a noble lot.

9 August

I was up at an early hour and in the course of the day we got 19. Ah, what a gift it was for me! . . . It turned to wet. Not much until I came to Aylsham and here I halted and got the pony fed and after tea I set off. I was not long on the road when it met me – I mean rain and thunder storms and lightning also, enough to frighten anyone.

When I arrived, I hardly ever saw my dear wife look worse as she is always afraid of the thunder and lightning. I put the pheasants out of the hampers. Went to bed and the storm abated, but I was sorry to say it again returned and woke us up.'

In spite of the difficulties with pheasant rearing, the season opened with a reasonable day's shooting. At the end of the day –

'the Honourable Sir T. F. Buxton, Bart. asked me did I still hold not to drink any beer or anything. My answer was, "Yes". "Then," said his honour, "here is a present for you, £1".

Ever since Larry had left Ireland as a young man, he had kept up a correspondence with Jacob Goff, the son of his first master in County Wexford. In July 1843 Larry had received a reply to his own letter written in late spring – a letter which had to be drafted twice for 'my wife tore it as I did not write humble enough'. The letter from Jacob Goff is transcribed into the diary.

'Horetown July 18 1843
Mr L. Banville
    I received your letter of the 5th in due course and would have replied to it, but have been much engaged with our assizes which have just terminated. The accounts in England relating to the state of this country are much exaggerated. A good deal of alarm has been caused on account of O'Connell going about and holding repeal meetings, but they all end quietly as no outrage has resulted from any of them as it is his intent to pursue peace and good order for if a rebellion was to break out, he would collect no more money which is his object in going about and holding those meetings which as yet have not been declared illegal or prevented by the government and which I think they ought to have done long since. I will send you by this day's post a Dublin paper and will occasionally send you one which will let you know the real state of affairs . . .
    I am building a great addition to my house. I have got on very well with it, but few others of the gentry of Ireland have charge to make any improvement or expend money in these times.
    However, I am not afraid . . .'

Once again, the whole of Ireland was consumed with resentment at the levying of Church tithes and O'Connell, now an old man, was making his final attempt to secure the repeal of the hated system. The promised newspaper reached Larry shortly after Jacob Goff's letter. From it he cut out an article describing the large incomes of the Irish Protestant bishops and pasted it into the diary.

In October Sir Fowell had a new experience in mind for Larry.

'I was glad to hear that my picture is to be drawn by this great man that is drawing the gentlemen at the Hall.

Thursday 12

I was obliged to stand to be drawn for the first time in my life. I was obliged to stand for two hours. I found it harder work to stand still for two hours than four hours hard walking in wet turnips.

Friday 13

I was at the Hall in the room for near four hours as he wanted to finish my picture and sure enough it was finished. Its appearance almost frightened me as my face was a dead red and my head just double the size it ever appeared to me in a glass. My arms as thick as the yard arm of a 74-gun man o'war ship and my legs appeared as thick as mill posts. All the servants said that it was my very self stuck up between two sticks which the drawer says it will stand good for ever. I hope that all will it see will think of me.'

Meanwhile, the sins of Mr and Mrs May were such that Larry determined to remove them by acquiring the lease of the other half of the Runton house which was the property of Mr Windham of Felbrigg.

'Mr Windham said I should pay him £3 for the other part of the house which that, of course, I agreed to do. It is let for one year so I shall have the house in spite of May and his favoured whore.'

A fortnight later, Banville felt obliged to tell Sir Fowell about one of May's particular misdemeanours.

'I shall tell the reader about the honesty of Mr May. He is taking up carrots for Sir T. F. Buxton and he takes full one quarter of them home for himself. What a shame it is! When I told it to Sir T. F. Buxton, he asked me if I was good friends with May. I told him for what I know I was, but I did not care who knows it as it was the truth.

Monday 20 November

This morning I met Gray, the gardener, who took a sample of the carrots that May takes home. Sir T. F. Buxton ordered them to be put into the earth and that he would speak about them another time . . . Mr May takes the men out of the plantations and makes them work for him half the day . . . This night I was told that May took a cart-load of posts and rails away belonging to Sir F., but I shall tell Sir F.'

At this point Buxton fell seriously ill. Larry thought he was dying.

'Sunday 3 December
I am in a deal of trouble about my master as he is very ill.

5 of the month
I saw Sir T. F. Buxton, Bart. I asked after his health, but his answer was he did a little better, but hardly could tell how he felt with a voice as weak as a child.

Monday the 11
. . . In the evening, at my return to the Hall, Sir T. F. Buxton, Bart. wished to speak to me when I would come in . . . What happened this night, it is as follows: her Ladyship came to me and ordered me out of the Hall so that they could tell my master I was gone . . . But it is all well with the rich here on earth, but woe to the rich tyrant. Her Ladyship is one. I believe I shall not see him more. He always was a friend of mine and that they did not like. But I leave it in the hands of the most high God to work it out for Poor Larry.

Tuesday 19
This morning up to the Hall. I there hear a poor account of Sir F. I then set off to shoot – 4 partridges, 2 hares, 3 rabbits was my sport. I was happy to see Sir T. F. Buxton in the chair that he was dragged about in. He spoke to me pretty cheerful.

I saw William Parsons this day who told me he would send for his brother James to come to see Sir T. F. Buxton which I wish he may come. There is two of my dear children playing crosspins, the same as children play in my mother country. They are as merry as crickets behind a turf fire in Ireland, but I can truly say my heart is sad.

Wednesday 20
. . . At my return to the Hall they told me that Sir F. was a deal better. I was so glad of the news, I left without my dinner to take the news to my wife. They also told me my picture was hanging in the drawing room. It is all past by me when I hear of Sir Fowell's health.

· Thursday 28

This morning up to the Hall. There I waited until 12 o'clock. At this moment I was told that Sir T. F. Buxton, Bart. was going out to a small covert to get a few shots. Now the reader must think what news it was to me. I can only say I believe if he was dead and rose again, my heart would not be more raised at that moment. He is in a small vehicle drawn by Sam [Banville], pushed by the others. At the covert, I was standing by his weak frame. It was weak indeed, but he stood at his old favoured spot. When Sir T. F. Buxton, Bart. shot the first pheasant, N. Buxton, Esq., cried out aloud, "Father, you have got straight powder." Then he run and picked it up. Ah! What I felt at that moment! I cannot tell what a joyful tale this is to me. I set off to Mrs Cook, also the coachman, and told it to them. They all was as glad as myself.'

> A week later, Sir Fowell felt well enough to turn his attention to the affair of May and the carrots.

'Thursday 4 January 1844
Sir T. F. Buxton, Baronet, told me that he was pretty well now and that he ne'er had any understanding about the carrots, but I told him that I thought he might wait a little longer as he was not well enough to stand the fatigue of it. He told me it made him right sick when he thought of it.

Saturday 6 January 1844
Sir T. F. Buxton, Baronet, sent for me to speak to in the dining-room. Strange to say it was for to give me five oranges for my children because I drank nothing. This very simple thing I thought more of it than if he had put his hand into his pocket and made me a present as he often done before as it showed great kindness. If he was let alone and all men dealt fair with Sir T. F. Buxton, Baronet, there would not be a better master in the kingdom.'

> Larry always suspected that his master would have preferred to have been left in ignorance of Mr May's thefts. It was nearly the end of February before the case was dealt with.

'Sir T. F. Buxton told me not to quarrel with May as I could not do a worse thing. My answer was I did not say anything but the truth and that I did not care who hear it. He told me to send my boy and a farmer to speak to him that seen it done.

Saturday 24 February
This day I went to Sir T. F. Buxton and he told me that the carrot story was to be brought up on Monday and that he did not wish me to come up to the Hall at all and that he wished that his servants did not see with such eyes as

they did. I was to stop in Cromer and if he wanted me, he would know where to send for me.

Monday 26 of February

This day, the men went up to the Hall to settle about the carrots. When Gray, the gardener of Sir T. F. Buxton, produced the carrots, Mr H. Johnson was there and he wanted to know who sent him to take the carrots out of the heap. They could not say that he was honest after all . . . But Sir T. F. Buxton forgave all.

Tuesday 27 February 1844

This morning I was at the Hall and at half past 9 o'clock the butler came to me. Told me to go in the garden to my master which I did and in his usual way, "How do you do this morning?" was his address to me. I shall write what took place as we walked arm in arm. "I am pleased," said he, "that you were not here yesterday. I am well satisfied that you did your duty." '

A few days later, Buxton, his wife and daughter Richenda, left No-threpps for Bath. There they joined Lady Buxton's sister, Elizabeth Fry, whose health was causing serious concern.

'This morning I set off to the Hall to witness the Baronet's departure and the old Lady and Miss Buxton. Now when he was going away, he shook hands with me and said, "Goodbye, Larry. I wish you well." '

Larry also said farewell to Samuel, his eldest son.

'Tuesday 2 April 1844

This was a day of great pleasure to me to see that Sir T.F.B., Bart. thought of my poor boy, Samuel, that he got him [a place] in the garden at Ham House in Essex.

Wednesday 3

Up at an early hour. Off to Norwich and my wife with me to send my son off to London and went off to the nursery of Mr Mackie's [where Samuel had been working] where they gave him a good word. He then got his wages and we went to his lodging and got tea. Then sent him on the coach for the City of London. I hope that it will be for his good, but he must see for himself as he have now near £20 in the bank which is a great help to him as he will have a shilling for a wet day. My dear wife and my son parted in a deal better spirits than I thought for, but she ne'er was with me before in the City [of Norwich] which was a great pleasure to me. This was a fine night. At a late hour, home safe at Springdale Valley.'

Chapter Sixteen

THE FAITHFUL SERVANT

1844–69

The last dated entries in the diary are for early May 1844. They show Banville absorbed once again in the game prospects for the coming season, discussing the best way to rear pheasants and characteristically grumbling about the behaviour of the keeper, Payne. There is no suggestion that he might discontinue his journal. After all, it was a great comfort to him that it was all 'to show the public at a future day'.

That there were further diaries kept is in little doubt, for Larry makes various references forward to items which he intends to include. Indeed, the last daily entry ends with Larry's intention to copy Buxton's reply to one of his letters. Moreover, it is most unlikely that a habit kept up so assiduously throughout his entire adult life should have stopped at this point. Perhaps the other diaries were part of that heap of rotting papers found in his attic after his death.

Larry and his master had not always seen eye to eye. The final disturbance had lasted many months and had been a serious upset felt keenly by Banville but less so by Buxton, who seemed largely unaware of Larry's distress. Yet the regard each felt for the other was clearly to be seen, especially in Larry's immediate readiness to put all his grievances aside when he feared his master was near death. Moreover, in their writings, the two men expressed their affectionate respect for each other: there were Larry's repeated reminders to his readers that his master was without equal – indeed, one of the last entries in the diaries described Buxton as 'one of the best masters in the kingdom'; there were Buxton's letters to his sons describing Larry's watchful care and amusing companionship on his various expeditions. What could have been more telling than Larry's amused remark in 1834:

'There is no one in the world have a better right to shoot poor Larry than his honour'?

Very little is known of Larry Banville after the final diary entry for 13 May 1844 in Volume IV, which is followed by a transcription of a letter he had written to his master in response to a request for local news and information about his success in hatching pheasants' eggs.

Sir Thomas Fowell Buxton died on 9 February 1845. In his description of the funeral, Lady Buxton's brother, Joseph John Gurney, wrote,

'He was buried in the ruined chancel of the little church at Overstrand. The old walls overrun with ivy, the building itself with the sea in full view, and the whole surrounding scenery, are highly picturesque.

The funeral, which was conducted with great simplicity, took place on a mild sunny winter's morning, and was attended by a large train of relatives, friends and neighbours. Long before the appointed hour crowds of villagers were seen approaching the spot, through the lanes and fields, in every direction. All seemed deeply moved'.

Who can doubt that Larry Banville was amongst them?

Overstrand Church. During the 18th century the building had fallen into decay. The Buxton tombs lie just outside the chancel at the east end of the church, and Larry's grave was to be placed just were the artist stood when drawing this picture.

[217]

There is no doubt that the diary of Larry Banville is an unusual document. Certainly there were other journals written by working people during the first half of the 19th century and, in fact, a flowering of soldiers' diaries was a feature of the Peninsula War. However, Larry's diary combines several fields of interest, each one of which has little comparable record during this period: that of an Irish immigrant, a gamekeeper and a member of the closely knit working community in North Norfolk – although his nationality, religion and job all combined to make it virtually impossible for him to be fully accepted by that community. He was also an experienced traveller in England, Ireland, Scotland and Sweden. He was the servant of two distinguished masters – the first widely known as a hunter and naturalist, the second as a philanthropist and social reformer.

The diary reveals Larry to have been a devoted and resourceful, loyal and hard-working servant. His outstanding qualities were recognized by Thomas Fowell Buxton early in their relationship and before long Larry became much more to the Buxton family than just an employee. His reliability and enterprise made him an

Anna Gurney in her invalid carriage at Overstrand. She is attended by her footmen Spinks and Stephen, and her companions are Hannah Buxton, Louisa Hoare and Amelia Carr. The sketch, by Anna Curtis, dates from 1844.

ideal man to entrust with the task of acquiring capercaillies and taking them to Scotland single-handed; while his amusing fund of anecdotes made him an amiable hunting companion. The references to him in the papers of T. F. Buxton show that he was regarded with fondness and esteem by the family and their friends. Even in his old age, the Buxton grandchildren were going to his cottage for tea, seeking his companionship and enjoying his stories.

Outwardly Larry kept tight control of himself even when physically assaulted, so the diary must have been a most effective means of releasing any pent-up feelings of anger and injustice. Moreover, he knew that once his writings were available for public scrutiny, he would be fully vindicated by his readers. He might give way to righteous indignation, but the overriding impression of him is of a man who was utterly dependable and honest at all times.

Of his family, very little is told in the diary. This was probably due to its being intended for publication and this, no doubt, accounts also for the deliberate cutting out of several of the entries either by Larry or some other person. It is obvious from the entry immediately before the missing sentences that some scandal is about to be reported. Other entries have been heavily scored through and it is often possible to decipher a piece of gossip beneath the lines or the report of a quarrel with his wife. He mentions his wife, Sarah, only infrequently and his children hardly at all.

It is interesting to see that on several occasions which were important to the Buxton family, notably the beginning of August 1833 when the Slavery Bill was being dealt with in the House of Commons, the relevant pages have been torn from the diary. It is impossible to say who removed these entries; perhaps it was Charles Buxton who used them as material for the biography he wrote of his father.

That Larry kept such a journal was widely known both amongst the Buxton, Hoare and Upcher families and by his local acquaintances. Larry mentioned that the Buxton children's governess asked to read his account of his Swedish travels and when Edward North Buxton wrote an article for the journal *Rural Sports* in 1840, documenting the re-introduction of capercaillies into Britain, in order to give colour to his account, he quoted sections of Larry's diary which described the collection of the birds in Sweden and their journey to Scotland. Larry's record was, however, heavily rewritten by Edward North Buxton.

There were a few blank pages at the end of the last volume of the diary and, in order not to waste space, Larry entered various financial accounts, game statistics and a copy of the inventory of gamekeeping items which he was obliged to compile on the death of his master. The latest date appearing in these various accounts is 1849–50 which is annotated 'the last year that I lived at Cromer . . . 1850 Runton, Norfolk'.

One or two glimpses of Larry's later life can be found in various scattered papers. His friendship with James Guthrie, Lord Breadalbane's gamekeeper, continued and they kept up the friendship begun in Scotland in 1836. At the beginning of January 1846, Guthrie wrote to him,

> 'the capercaillies are still doing well at Taymouth, and abound in great numbers. This last summer did not answer for their young, on account of the wetness of the season – still a good many of them came through. A man can easily see from forty to fifty broods in a day, at the breeding season – so you can judge, if the one half of these were to come through, there would be an increase of two or three hundred. We have shot none this season and I have heard of none being shot.
>
> Lord Glenlyon's gamekeeper informs me that they have got a great many in the woods at Dunkeld. Several other gentlemen have got a few, but not many – there are but few gentlemen that have woods to answer for them in Scotland'.

In August 1857, Larry was interviewed by Henry Stevenson, the famous Norfolk ornithologist, who was collecting material for his first comprehensive book on the *Birds of Norfolk*. According to Stevenson's diary, Larry recounted the details of his journeys from Sweden with the capercaillies. Larry also told him how he –

> 'tried to rear Black Grouse at Beeston, but though the soil was well suited and the heaths, hills and fern with fir plantations, just the thing, yet the open space is too confined, the valleys too near each other, to admit of those long flights undisturbed which those birds delight in'.

When Stevenson's book was published in 1866. he included a summary of the information given him by Larry – '"Old Larry" to those Cromer visitors who "picnic" on the Beeston Hills'. In his book Stevenson also mentions a letter from Henry Upcher which neatly finishes off the story of those capercaillies brought to Norfolk by Larry: the one bird remaining after Buxton's gift to Prince Albert was turned out into Sheringham woods.

This drawing by Ellen Buxton, Thomas Fowell's grand-daughter, shows Larry by his fireside. It is annotated 'Larry sitting in his cottage listening to Anna reading to him the life of Sir E. Parry – Jan. 8 1866'.

'He lived for about six months and then was found dead with a fir-cone stuck in his throat. He had a collar with his direction round his throat which probably was the cause of his choking'.

Larry appears briefly in the notebooks of Ellen Buxton, Thomas Fowell's grand-daughter. She writes of him, an old man in his cottage at Runton, and draws him by his fireside. The drawing shows Larry with a cloth wrapped round his right hand. It is possible that his hand is covered or protected as the result of a stroke which had left some paralysis.

Ellen Buxton's references show that he was a popular figure with the children.

'Thursday 9 October 1861
We had tea outside the door of Larry's cottage. Mrs Banville supplied us with eggs, hot water, and two or three other little necessaries . . .

A photograph taken in 1864 of gamekeepers at Banville's cottage, Runton. Larry, standing second from the left, is seen holding a woodcock. The figure second on the right is possibly Larry's youngest son, Henry, usually known as Larry the Second. In front of the group lie partridges and pheasants. The 19th-century brick-built cottage is thatched with Norfolk reeds. It is still standing but unoccupied.

Tuesday 24 February 1863

. . . in the afternoon we all packed into the carriage and poneych-air and went to Runton to pick primroses . . . We got a great many primroses and then went and made a call on Larry and Mrs Banville, Larry, of course, amusing us by his talk all the time'.

Larry accompanied the children on fishing expeditions. They dug ferns from his garden and feasted on his apples. On another occasion at the end of the summer of 1863, Larry was asked to help search for a child's watch lost on the hills and on 5 November greatly pleased the Buxton grandchildren who were staying at Northrepps Hall.

'The boys set to work to scoop out the largest turnip I ever saw in my life which Larry had brought them to make a Guy Fawkes . . . We are going to stick a candle in it and perhaps put it in the garden in the evening.'

Larry's diaries continued to be important to him. When he made his will in 1858, he directed his executors 'to place into the possession of Charles Buxton Esq. and Buxton Johnston Esq. [the son and grandson of Thomas Fowell] all and every my Diary Manuscripts and Papers which I wish to be published'.

Larry died in 1869 – from a stroke, according to his death certificate. Charles Buxton died two years later and the diaries were never published until now. Yet the Buxton family always remembered Larry. They placed a brass plaque on the south wall of East Runton church. It reads – in its original spelling –

'To Lawrence Banvill
for nearly 50 years the faithful and respected servant
of the first Sir T. F. Buxton, Bart. and his family
by whom this tablet is erected.
He died March 23rd 1869 aged about 73 years.
"Therefore being justified by faith, we have peace with God
through our Lord Jesus Christ."'

ACKNOWLEDGEMENTS

We would like to thank Verily Paget, June Ross, Lena Andrew, Anthony Johnson, Martin Warren of Cromer Museum, Amanda Parry, and David Dawson of Anglia Television for their help; Kirsty Chreighton for allowing the reproduction of entries and a drawing from *Ellen Buxton's Diary*; and Priscilla Gill, Henry Buxton, Norwich Record Office and Local History Library, Norwich Castle Museum and Thodes House Library, Oxford, for permission to publish extracts from documents in their care.

PICTURE CREDITS

COLOUR *Facing page;*

32 both, 81, 128 above, 192 both, 193 Mary Evans Picture Library

16, 33, 96 both, 112 above, 136 both, 144, 145, 201; between pp. 200–201 Lord Buxton

40 both, 64, 113 below, 137, 177 above, 200; between pp. 40–41, 136–7 Norfolk Museums Service (Norwich Castle Museum)

41, 113 above, 129 The Executors, Sheringham Hall

65 Verily Paget

17 BBC Hulton Picture Library

80 both, 128 below, 176; between pp. 200–201 left, both, John Southern

97 The Mansell Collection

177 below Norma Virgoe

193 below Reproduced by gracious permission of HM The Queen

BLACK AND WHITE *Page:*

15, 34, 35, 87, 222 Lord Buxton

23, 43, 69, 185, 205 BBC Hulton Picture Library

36, 59, 62, 76, 106, 120 Norfolk Museums Service (Norwich Castle Museum)

38, 111 Henry Buxton (*Photographed by Nicolette Hallett*)

51 *Field Sports of the North of Europe* Llewelyn Lloyd

57, 66, 77, 90, 99, 103, 125 both, 143, 146, 163, 195 Mary Evans Picture Library

61, 126, 150, 194 The Mansell Collection

102, 217 *The Gurneys of Earlham* Augustus Hare

127 Dick Joice

138 *Memorials of Hannah, Lady Buxton* C.E.B.

139, 218 Norfolk Museums Service (Cromer Museum)

171 Arvika Museum, Sweden

173 *Game Birds and Wild Flow of Sweden and Norway* Llewelyn Lloyd

181 Norma Virgoe

188 National Portrait Gallery

221 Kirsty Chreighton